Studying in English

A practical approach to study skills in English as a second language

J B Heaton

Longman

Longman Group Limited
London

*Associated companies, branches and representatives throughout the
world*

©Longman Group Ltd 1975

First published 1975
. New impression 1978
ISBN 0 582 55205 2

Filmset by Keyspools Limited, Golborne, Lancashire
Printed in Hong Kong by
Sing Cheong Printing Co Ltd

Contents

Unit Ten
Learning and remembering

Unit Eleven
Examinations

Unit Twelve
Reference and research techniques

Bibliography   99

Appendix: Talks and lectures (Scripts)

Unit Seven
Reading textbooks

Unit Eight
Learning in small groups: Tutorials and seminars

Unit Nine
Writing reports and articles

Unit Ten
Learning and remembering

Unit Eleven
Examinations

Unit Twelve
Reference and research techniques

Foreword

Students whose mother tongue is not English meet many new problems when they start studying at universities and colleges where English is the medium of instruction. Some of them find that the variety of English they have learned is literary and old-fashioned. Some of them have read very little English about the subjects they are studying. Few of them are expert silent readers, and the skills they have are often appropriate only for the reading of simple fiction and not suited to the study of textbooks and journals written in scholarly English. They have all learned to write compositions but not to compose reports and articles. They may never have been taught how to make notes from books or lectures or even how to listen efficiently to talks and lectures. These are only a few of the tasks which are essential for studying in universities and colleges but to which many students have given little time while they were at school.

It is hoped, therefore, that this book will prove useful not only for the first-year student at college or university but also for the sixth-form student who intends to continue with his studies in the medium of English. An increasing number of books now being published will assist the student to master the particular varieties of English he will require. This book is intended to develop the language skills he will need.

The practice material is arranged in units and may be used in class by the teacher or on a self-instruction basis. Each unit contains two or three hours' work, concentrating on developing the listening, note-taking, and reading skills. Listening comprehension and note-taking are practised in every unit, while practice in reading alternates with practice in listening to lectures. Writing practice is also included in each unit, the 'model' notes for each lecture and reading text providing a basis for writing. Both teacher and student will find that the note-taking practice given in the book provides a useful means of teaching writing.

This book functions in two ways simultaneously: it provides useful information and practical hints on how to study in the medium of English and at the same time practises wherever possible the techniques advocated. For example, in one unit the student hears a short lecture concerning ways of improving his reading ability while in the next unit he reads a text about listening to lectures. Exercises on each of the skills described are also given in the Practice section of each unit. All the major study skills, therefore, are reinforced through constant practice. Since the contents of each talk, lecture and reading text concentrate solely on study techniques, a degree of cohesion of subject matter is attained, making it possible for the material to be used with students of the sciences as well as students of the arts. It is hoped, therefore, that students of all disciplines will find the book equally interesting and useful.

A tape has been produced to accompany the book. However, many lecturers and teachers will undoubtedly wish to use the book without feeling dependent on a tape-recorder. Consequently, the scripts of all the talks and lectures are included in the Appendix and may be either read aloud to the class or treated as a reading text. The tape-recording, however, is advantageous for students who are working on their own and who otherwise will miss the listening practice.

Acknowledgements

I wish to express my sincere thanks to Mr A K Pugh for his advice and encouragement during the writing of this book and during our frequent discussions on learning techniques, particularly on the development of the reading skills. Indeed, many of the terms used in the sections on reading have been adopted from the conceptual framework outlined by Mr Pugh in 'The development of silent reading' in *The Road to Effective Reading*, ed. D W Latham. Ward Lock, London, 1974.

I also wish to express my gratitude to Mr John Bright for his extremely useful comments and constructive suggestions on earlier drafts.

JBH

We are grateful to the following for permission to reproduce copyright material: The Clarendon Press for the definition of the word 'study' from *The Concise Oxford Dictionary* 5th edition 1965; Longman Group Ltd for the definition of the word 'study' from the *New Method Dictionary* and for an extract from *Overseas Students' Companion to English Studies* by J B Heaton and J P Stocks: G & C Merriam Company for the definition of the word 'study' from *Webster's Third New International Dictionary.* © 1971 by G & C Merriam Co., Publishers of the Merriam Webster Dictionaries: Oxford University Press for the definition of the word 'study' from *Advanced Learner's Dictionary of Current English.* © Oxford University Press 1971 and from *Oxford Advanced Learner's Dictionary of Current English.* © Oxford University Press 1974: Penguin Books Ltd for an extract from *What's The Use of Lectures?* by Donald Bligh. © Donald A Bligh, 1972 and Scott, Foresman & Company for an excerpt from the introduction to *Thorndike-Barnhart Comprehensive Desk Dictionary* by Clarence L Barnhart. © 1962 by Scott, Foresman and Company. Reprinted by permission of Scott, Foresman and Company.

Unit One
Study problems and objectives

A Listening comprehension: Study problems

Listen carefully to the talk which you are about to hear. Answer each question below *when you are instructed to do so.*

Study Problems

1 According to what you have just heard, write T if the following statement is true or F if it is false:
   Generally study problems are more serious for foreign learners than for native speakers.

2 Complete the following sentence by writing one word to replace each blank:
   Sometimes students confuse study problems with _____ or _____ problems.

3 Choose the best answer, *a, b* or *c*:
   Language is often a serious problem in studying at advanced levels because
   a a more literary kind of English is now required.
   b the classroom variety of English learnt at school is unsuitable.
   c the student is now required to read more artificial textbooks.

4 You will now hear about the language skills or abilities which you will need in your study. Listen carefully and write down the listening and speaking skills which you will require.

5 Complete the following sentence by writing one word to replace each blank:
   The student is expected to _____ widely and to _____ for himself at college or university level.

B Note-taking: Word omissions

General

Words can be divided into two broad classes: *content* words and *form* words. Content words are generally nouns, adjectives, verbs and (most) adverbs; form words are the words which are used to provide the pattern or framework of the sentence. In the following sentence, for example, the form words are *There, is, an, of, the*, and *of*:

There is an increasing awareness of the importance of correct study habits.

It is often possible to omit form words in notes (eg auxiliaries, determiners, pronouns). Since these words form the framework of sentences, many can be omitted without consequent loss of meaning. Such words, in fact, are usually omitted in telegrams as well as in notes. Look at the following sets of content words: it is possible to guess the general pattern of the sentence in which each set originally appeared. (Note that dashes are frequently used to denote missing form words.)

i   Increasing awareness – importance correct study habits.

ii Book – possible practise skills needed.

   = In this book it is possible to practise the skills that are needed.

iii Language required (by) student – different (from) classroom English learnt.

   = The language which is required by the student will now be very different from the classroom kind of English he learnt.

Words often omitted

1 *Be, have,* and *do*

   a *Be, have* and *do* as auxiliaries are usually omitted in notes, especially when there are other indications of tense: present/past participle forms (eg study*ing*, studi*ed*), prepositions (eg about, over), adverbs (eg quickly, carefully) and adverbial groups (eg at a fast pace), etc.

         The student ∧ performing different language tasks when he takes notes.

         Students at university or college ∧ certain advantages over younger students at school.

         Most students ∧ not realise that study problems exist.

   b *Be* can be omitted when it denotes the passive (eg English *is spoken* a lot in Singapore).

         Syllabuses, examinations and teaching ∧ all largely determined by literary values.

   c When followed by a noun/a pronoun/an adjective, *be* is often replaced by the sign =.

         Study problems = major difficulties to many foreign learners.

2 *Noun determiners*

   Unless there is danger of ambiguity, omit *a, an, the* and *some* in notes.

      ∧ More familiar ∧ student is with ∧ particular subject, ∧ easier he will cope with ∧ university course.

3 *Formal/Impersonal subjects*

   There is/There are and the impersonal *It* used as a substitute subject can be omitted without loss of meaning.

      There are two kinds of approaches to study: the positive kind _____

Two kinds of approaches to study: positive _____

It is impossible to be successful unless the student thinks for himself.

Impossible be successful unless student thinks for himself.

4 *Personal pronouns*

    a Pronouns (*I, me, my, mine, myself*, etc) are omitted in notes if (i) there is no ambiguity and (ii) the pronouns are not used to denote an important contrast.

        Many of the problems are not wholly language ones. They are chiefly study problems.

        Many problems – not wholly language = chiefly study problems.

    b *We, you* and *one* used in an impersonal or general sense are omitted in notes.

        We learn the most complex skill of all when we are young children: we learn to speak.

        Learn most complex skill when young children = to speak.

5 *Nouns and noun groups*

The same or identical nouns are often used by speakers to refer back, thus linking ideas and providing cohesion and continuity. Such words (which merely repeat information) can generally be omitted in notes.

    Note-taking involves more than aural comprehension and the ability to retain information. Note-taking is, in fact, a complex series of skills.

    Note-taking = more than aural comprehension & retention = complex series of skills.

6 *Miscellaneous word omissions*

The following can also be omitted in notes:

    a relative pronouns (*that, which, whom*) when they are objects in adjectival clauses.

        The language that a student requires will differ in certain ways from the textbook kind of English which the student learnt at school.

        Language student requires = different from textbook English learnt at school.

    b *of the* in phrases like *most of the, all of the, many of the*, etc.

        Many of the language skills that are required now were not practised at school.

        Many language skills required now – not practised at school.

    c *to* when used to introduce an infinitive.

        The ability to take notes is a skill which is often neglected.

        Ability take notes = skill often neglected.

    d prepositions indicating time, direction, place (eg *at, in, on*) and those prepositions which can normally be inferred from the verb/adjective/noun (eg *forget about, aim at, interested in, certain of, similar to*).

It is important for each student to obtain a rough idea of his progress at regular intervals.

Important each student obtains idea of progress regular intervals.

C Reading: Study objectives

Read the following text as fast as you can in order to obtain a general idea of the content. The maximum time allowed for each section is 1 minute.

Section 1

The first step in developing effective methods of study is for the student to establish worthwhile but realistic objectives. These goals must be neither too easy nor too difficult to attain: goals which are easy offer the student very little incentive to make any real effort since they neither stimulate interest nor give rise to the feelings of satisfaction which result from having achieved something worthwhile. Most people, for example, tend to play badly in a game against a poor opponent but play well against a good opponent: the poor opponent offers little competition but the good opponent brings out the best in the other player by forcing him to increase his concentration and effort. In setting goals, most people use past experience as their chief guide, increasing their expectations slightly each time a goal is achieved. In fact, determining a particular goal is linked very closely with confidence as well as with motivation. While those who have failed badly in the past may try harder in future, repeated failure only discourages. If, therefore, the student fails to achieve several of his goals, he should consider lowering his sights and setting more realistic goals for himself.

True/False

Now write T if each statement is true according to the writer and F if it is false or untrue.

1 In order to begin to study efficiently, it is necessary to have realistic goals.
2 Objectives which are easy to achieve are the most effective ones in steadily improving study techniques.
3 A good player in any game tends to make his opponent try harder and thus play better.
4 After having achieved one of their goals, most people generally make their next goal slightly easier.
5 Students should never lower their goals even if they fail to attain them.

Instead of

Look carefully again at the text in order to complete the following statements. Give the actual words the writer uses.

6 Instead of saying that easy goals do not encourage the student to try hard, the writer says that easy goals provide the student with _____

7 Instead of saying that a good opponent makes the other player play as well as he can, the writer says that a good opponent _____

8 Instead of saying that most people hope they can do even better the next time after achieving their goal, the writer says that they increase _____

9 Instead of saying that forming a certain goal depends on how confident and interested a person is in a subject, the writer says that forming a goal is _____

10 Instead of saying that a student loses his enthusiasm if he constantly fails, the writer says that _____

Section 2

The goals set can be divided into two groups: intermediate or short-term objectives and long-term objectives. Short-term objectives concern individual units of work: contributing to a tutorial, the research necessary to write a report, etc. Written assignments set by tutors can be regarded as valuable intermediate objectives, offering a sense of purpose and direction to the student. Long-term objectives concern such goals as the attainment of the particular knowledge and skills required to perform an appropriate task successfully – often, in more concrete terms, preparation for an end-of-course examination or the completion of a thesis. Clearly maximum progress will take place only when the short-term objectives are related both to one another and to a long-term objective.

True/False

Now write T if each statement is true according to the writer and F if it is false or untrue.

11 There are three kinds of goals: intermediate, short-term, and long-term goals.

12 An example of a short-term goal is the preparation necessary in order to write a report.

13 Written assignments are not too useful because they usually discourage students.

14 The writer refers to examinations and theses as examples of long-term objectives.

15 It is important to relate short-term goals to a long-term objective.

Instead of

Look carefully again at the text in order to complete the following statements. Give the actual words the writer uses.

16 Instead of saying that goals can be classified according to whether they are short-term objectives or long-term ones, the writer says that goals can be_____

17 Instead of saying that preparation for a tutorial or a report is an example of a short-term goal, the writer says that _____

18 Instead of describing written assignments as providing helpful guide-lines for the student, the writer says that they _____

19 Instead of talking about *obtaining* knowledge and skills for a certain task, the writer uses the phrase _____ of knowledge.

20 Instead of saying that short-term objectives must be linked to long-term ones before the student can work at his most efficient, the writer says that _____

Section 3

It is important for each student to obtain at regular intervals a rough idea of his progress. How are goals being achieved week by week? Methods of continuous assessment of students' work are replacing examinations – or parts of examinations – on certain courses. There are still doubts about the advantages of continuous assessment in the learning process but, if applied with care and discretion, continuous assessment can be a far more valuable means of assessing standards than an examination. Provided that methods of continuous assessment do not impart a feeling of tension and strain, they can be used to guide the student in his work and to inform him of the progress he is making. If no means of continuous assessment is available, the student should attempt to evaluate and summarise very briefly his progress week by week. Clearly, such an attempt is more difficult in a subject which teaches skills (eg learning a language, playing a musical instrument) than in a content subject (eg history, chemistry). Even as far as skills are concerned, however, it is a simple matter for the student to go back to an old exercise and do it again. The ease with which he can do what previously seemed a difficult exercise is often quite remarkable.

True/False

Now write T if each statement is true according to the writer and F if it is false or untrue.

21 The student will benefit if he is made aware of his progress from time to time.

22 All educationalists are now aware of the advantages of continuous assessment.

23 Examinations are inferior to continuous assessment provided that the latter is used with care and discretion.

24 Each week it is helpful for students to write a summary of the progress they feel they have made.

25 It is unwise for students to repeat old exercises even though they may seem simple.

Instead of

Look carefully again at the text in order to complete the following statements. Give the actual words the writer uses.

26 Instead of referring to ways of measuring at regular intervals a student's progress, the writer uses the phrase _____

27 Instead of talking about using such methods carefully and wisely, the writer talks about applying them _____

28 Instead of saying that continuous assessment is useful unless it makes the student feel upset and worried, the writer says that it is useful _____

29 Instead of saying that the student should try to assess and report briefly on his progress every week, the writer says that _____

30 Instead of saying that it is harder for the student to assess progress made in learning a language than in history, the writer says that _____

Section 4

Another important factor in the achievement of one's goals is motivation. Motivation may result from an interest in the subject being studied or even from simply the desire to get a degree. It is rare, however, to find motivation which does not have some interest in the subject as its basis, and the student should be aware of those areas or subjects which do not interest him. He should search for ways in which he can pursue his objectives in the particular way of most interest to him. Relationships between branches of learning abound; and the student who finds himself lacking interest in a particular topic or subject should seek ways of relating this to an area which does interest him. Moreover, if he can stand back from time to time and look at the subject as a whole, he may well develop an interest in that individual part which he previously found uninteresting. A former British prime minister once said, 'The art of life is to make uninteresting parts into an interesting whole.' This is also true of study.

True/False

Now write T if each statement is true according to the writer and F if it is false or untrue.

31 Motivation generally results from at least some degree of interest in a subject.

32 It is generally sufficient if a student is motivated solely by a strong desire to obtain a degree or an equivalent qualification.

33 Students should try to work in the way which they find of most interest to them.

34 Attempts to see how an uninteresting subject is related to an interesting one may increase motivation.

35 It is rarely useful to take a broad view of the whole subject from time to time in the hope of increasing one's interest in a small part of it.

Instead of

Look carefully again at the text in order to complete the following statements. Give the actual words the writer uses.

36 Instead of saying that interest is also important in attaining one's objectives, the writer says that _____

37 Instead of saying that motivation almost always arises from an interest in the subject, the writer says that it is rare _____

38 Instead of advising the student to look for interesting methods and approaches in studying a subject, the writer says that _____

39 Instead of saying that subjects are connected with one another in many ways, the writer says that _____

40 Instead of advising the student to view occasionally the whole subject from a distance, the writer urges him to _____

Section 5

Furthermore, active participation generally leads to added interest in a particular subject or topic. Taking notes, writing critical comments on texts read, lively participation in seminars, all help to foster interest and understanding. Even the translation of a short text from English into the mother tongue (whatever merits or faults it may have as an exercise for language practice) helps to focus concentration and add interest.

It is generally all too easy to adopt a passive approach to study or to postpone study periods until a more 'suitable' time. Some students decide to wait until they are in the mood to study. This can be fatal: always start straight away. In his book *The Psychology of Study** C A Mace, while recommending rest periods and regular relaxation to guard against fatigue, warns against postponing study on account of initial inertia.

'Felt disinclinations to start work can be dealt with more ruthlessly. Here, if anywhere, is the case for the exercise of "will power", but will power can be supplemented by innocent devices of self-manipulation. A useful instrument for the control of felt disinclination is the timetable.'

The timetable is indeed a valuable instrument in helping to initiate and develop effective methods of study. The next unit will deal with study habits and with timetables.

True/False

Now write T if each statement is true according to the writer and F if it is false or untrue.

41 Motivation can be increased if the student has an active approach to his studies.

42 Taking notes tends to reduce a person's interest in a subject.

43 Concentration and interest can be increased through translation.

44 A student who finds it difficult to commence working should have a short period during which he can relax.

45 Timetables are useful for helping the student to begin work and to develop good habits of study.

Instead of

Look carefully again at the text in order to complete the following statements. Give the actual words the writer uses.

*C A Mace *The Psychology of Study*. Penguin, 1968.

46 Instead of saying that the student will become more interested the more he actually *does* while studying, the writer says that _____
47 Instead of referring to active and interesting discussion in seminars, the writer talks about _____
48 Instead of saying that translation can make students concentrate more and become more interested, the writer says that translation _____
49 Instead of talking about the temptation to put off study until a more 'suitable' time, C A Mace uses the phrase _____
50 Instead of talking about self-discipline in studying, C A Mace uses the phrase _____

Note-taking practice
Now re-read the complete text carefully and make notes.

NOTES

Study Objectives
1. Establish effective goals : if too easy – little incentive to make effort [e.g. games]; if too hard – discourage.

2. Short-term [intermediate] goals: e.g. research for writing report. Long-term goals – attain skills : e.g. examination, thesis.

3. Important to know progress made. Continuous assessment or weekly summary of progress – valuable. [Skills –difficult, but do old exercises again to see progress.]

4. Motivation: interest in subject important. Pursue goals in interesting way – relate uninteresting area to interesting one or look at subject as whole.

5. Active participation adds to interest : e.g. taking notes, translation.

6. Do not postpone study : initial inertia overcome by will-power. Timetable – useful. [C.A.Mace : Psychology of Study.]

Writing practice
Use the notes to write a brief account of the importance of formulating effective goals in following a university or college course. Mention the importance of motivation in any programme of study.

D   Practice section

Complete a questionnaire about your studies similar to the one shown here.

1 Course   i   Main course _____

            ii   Subsidiary course(s) _____

2 Goals   i   Long-term goal(s) _____

            ii   Short-term goal(s)_____

3 Progress   i   How is your achievement on the course assessed?
(Put a tick in the appropriate space.)

                  a   by examination   —

                  b   by continuous assessment   —

                  c   by both of these methods   —

            ii   Self-evaluation: assess the progress you have made (during
the preceding fortnight).

                  Method used _____

                  Progress   Good   —

                                      Fair   —

                                      Negligible   —

                  Remarks_____

4 Motivation   i   State the chief factors you feel assist your own motivation.

                  _____

            ii   Interest in subject(s) High   —

                                   Medium   —

                                     Low   —

                  Reasons for interest _____

           iii   Do you find any of the subjects you are studying lacking in

                  interest? (If so, state why.)_____

                  How do you think you can increase your interest in these

                  subjects?_____

5 Active   i Note-taking: Do you experience any difficulty in taking
  participation   notes during lectures?

                                           Yes/No

                           If your answer above was 'Yes', indicate what you feel is
                           most appropriate (*a* or *b*):
                           a Is the difficulty caused chiefly by a lack of ability to
                                understand lectures in English?

                                           —

                           b Can you understand the lectures but are nevertheless
                                unable to take useful notes? (Eg your notes are too long;
                                you cannot identify the important points on which to
                                base your notes.)

                                           —

                       ii Seminars: How much do you contribute in seminars?

                                    A lot   —

                                    Average   —

                                    Only a little   —

6 Timetable   Do you keep a timetable of your study?

                                           Yes/No

Now discuss your answers to this questionnaire with your friends or colleagues. After
revising your answers where necessary, write a brief report about your study habits
and objectives.

Unit Two
Organising your study

A Listening comprehension: Concentration and study habits

Listen carefully to the talk which you are about to hear. Answer each question below *when you are instructed to do so*.

Concentration and study habits

1 Replace each of the blanks:
   Three factors involved in concentration are:
   a individual differences
   b the nature of the __ __ (2 words)
   c __ (1 word)

2 Choose the best answer, *a, b* or *c*:
   In order to gain interest in a subject which does not interest us, we should attempt to:
   a increase our span of attention in the subject.
   b remember information when studying the subject.
   c relate the subject to something we find interesting.

3 Complete the following sentence by writing one word to replace each blank:
   Clearly defined objectives together with a sense of urgency may help to overcome problems of i _____ i: _____.

4 Complete the following sentence according to what you have just heard. (Write several words.)
   The more advanced the field of study, _____

5 According to what you have just heard, write T if the following statement is true or F if it is false:
   Study periods which involve the memorisation of a lot of information should be longer than those involving practical work.

B Note-taking: Abbreviations and numbers

1 *Abbreviations*

   a Some useful abbreviations are:
cf = compare; eg = for example; etc = and so on; ie = that is;
nb = note well; pp = pages; viz = namely.

   b Writing only the first part of many words is one common method of
abbreviating. (Note that full stops after abbreviations are frequently
omitted in notes.)

approx	approximately
encl	enclosed, enclosure
exam	examine, examination
transf	transfer
incl	including, inclusive
is	island
indep	independent
lab	laboratory, labour
lang	language
lit	literature
mag	magazine
ref	(with) reference (to)
geog	geography
hist	history
chem	chemistry
maths	mathematics
engrng	engineering
masc	masculine
soc	social, society
vocab	vocabulary

In order to avoid ambiguity, the last letter is frequently included in the
abbreviation:

amt	amount
dept	department
govt	government

   c Another method of reducing the length of words in note-taking is to omit all
or some of the vowels in the word or in part of the word. (It is generally not a
difficult matter to recognise words from which the vowels have been omitted:
eg vwls nd cnsnnts.)

favrd	favoured
attentn	attention
developmt	development
environmt	environment

d   Single letter abbreviations can be used to refer to words which have recently appeared in the notes.

> After making long-term plans, the students is then able to organise his short-term goals in the form of a timetable. Such a timetable must be based at the very outset on the student's knowledge of himself and his capabilities.
>
> 1 Student makes long-term plans.
> 2 Organises short-term goals in timetable. T – based on knowl of self and capabilities.

2 *Numbers*

In note-taking it is usually quicker to write figures than words for numbers.

> 321   (*not* three hundred and twenty-one) $\frac{1}{2}$ (*not* a half)

However, it is easier to write words than figures when there is a series of noughts.

> 7 million   (*not* 7,000,000) $14\frac{1}{2}$ m.   (*not* 14,500,000)

Note Abbreviate a word only if you think you can understand it later.

C Lecture: Planning a timetable

NOTES

Planning a Timetable

1. Many dislike strict timetables or prefer work in cycles.
2. But t = means of reaching goals thr regular work
   e.g. 1 hr a day – 5 days a wk [cf Chinese fable].
3. Long-term gls and short-term gls determine t.
     Don't overrate speed of prgrss.
     Make t after 1st week.
4. How long on study?
     Depends on t.   Ave stdnt – 40-50 hrs study a wk.
                     Arts   – 15 lctrs + 35 study.
                     Sc   – 25 lctrs + 25 study.
5. When to study?
     a) Morning – prob best.
        Night   – few distrctns
                – also slight body ftgue = good, but bad
                  if st = tired in morning.
     b) Plan study prd after lecture
                       before seminar.
6. Value of rest prds.
     a) Sats and Suns
     b) 'rewards' – cinema, etc.
     c) short breaks when tired or bored
     d) sleep = nec.
     Qlty —— not qnty— of study = imp.

Writing practice
Use the notes to write a short letter to a friend or colleague, giving him advice on planning a timetable of study.

D Practice section

1 In the light of what you have learnt about study methods in this unit, comment on the following timetable of a student studying Zoology as his main subject.

	Mon	Tues	Wed	Thur	Fri	Sat	Sun
8-9	Phys		Phys		Phys	Prac work:	↑
9-10	Anat	Zool	Anat	Zool	Bot		
10-11			Bot	↑	Anat	Zool	
11-12	Bot	Anat	Phys	[Bot]	[Anat]		
12-1	[Phys]	[Anat]		↓			FREE
1-2	LUNCH						
2-3	Phys	Prac work:	Prac work:		Prac work:	[Sport]	
3-4	[Anat]	Zool	Phys	Sem: Zool	Bot		
4-5	Sem: Bot						
5-6	[Bot]						
6-7	DINNER						
7-8			↑		[Anat]	[Film]	↓
8-9		[Anat]	[Free]	[Bot]			↑
9-10	[Phys]				[Phys]		[Zool]
10-11							↓
11-12	[Bot]	[Zool]	↓	[Zool]			
12-1							

The use of brackets in this timetable denotes private study periods (to distinguish from lectures). All the other periods take the form of lectures unless denoted otherwise (ie labelled *Seminar (Sem)*, *Practical work (Prac work)*, etc.

Key   Phys = Physiology   Anat = Anatomy
        Zool = Zoology   Bot   = Botany

2 The following timetable shows the lectures, tutorials and practical work of a 1st year student of Computer Science. Complete the timetable by putting in 20 hours of study periods.

	Mon	Tues	Wed	Thurs	Fri	Sat	Sun
9-10	C.P.	B.A.	C.P.	Stats	B.A.	C.P.	
10-11	Stats	Stats	A.Maths	Tutorl: P. Maths	Stats		
11-12							
12-1	P.Maths	A.Maths	P.Maths	A.Maths	P.Maths	English	
1-2							
2-3		Pract	Lang		English		
3-4	Tutorl: C.P.	Work:	Lab:	Tutorl: A Maths			
4-5		C.P.	English				
5-6	English			English	English		
6-7							
7-8							
8-9							
10-11							
11-12							
12-1							

Key   C P   = Computer Programming
      B A   = Boolean Algebra
      A Maths = Applied Mathematics
      P Maths = Pure Mathematics
      Stats   = Statistics
      Tutorl   = Tutorial

3 Draw up a timetable for your own study periods and write a few comments on the completed timetable, showing the various principles underlying it. The following points will be of help to you:
   a Those subjects which you find the most difficult should be given a lot of time in your timetable.
   b Sufficient time should also be allocated in your timetable to those subjects requiring considerable reading.

c Wherever possible, time should be given to appropriate study immediately *after* a lecture and immediately *before* a seminar.

d The use of a library or other suitable place of study should be considered when arranging study periods during the day.

e A decision should be made at the outset concerning the amount of time to be spent on hobbies and leisure activities.

Unit Three
Note-taking

A Listening comprehension: General principles of note-taking

Listen carefully to the talk which you are about to hear. Answer each question below *when you are instructed to do so.*

General principles of note-taking

1 Complete the following sentences by writing several words:
  a The weakest ink is superior to _____
  b Note-taking helps _____
2 According to what you have just heard, write T if the following statement is true or F if it is false:
  Note-taking is beneficial because it helps the student to participate actively in learning.
3 Complete the sentence by writing several words:
  The amount of notes taken during a lecture is determined by the type of lecture and _____
4 Choose the best answer, *a, b* or *c*:
  Detailed notes are usually of little help because
  a they fail to distinguish between important and unimportant points.
  b most students have insufficient time to remember all the details.
  c it is possible to read all the points in a book.
5 Complete the following sentence by writing one word to replace each blank:
  When taking notes from a book, it is possible to work from the _____ to the _____; however, when taking notes during a lecture, it is necessary to work from the _____ to the _____.
6 The speaker warns against copying out notes neatly. What does he advise? (Write a sentence.)
7 Write T if the following statement is true or F if it is false:
  Translation of lectures into the student's mother tongue is recommended during note-taking.

B Note-taking: Salient points

In the initial stages of learning to take notes, key words and phrases assume great importance as a means of deducing the meaning of a series of utterances. It is helpful to practise listening for the salient points in short talks. Such salient points are often shown by emphasis, repetition or simply a slowing down in the pace of delivery. Concentration of attention on such points will help to prevent notes from becoming shorthand renderings of a talk or lecture. Consequently, although an ability to omit words and to use abbreviations is essential for note-taking purposes, equally important is the more positive approach of attempting to identify salient points by distinguishing the relevant from the irrelevant or less relevant.

The following examples show how several sentences can be reduced to one line of notes:

1 Some lecturers approach certain subjects with a degree of bias or prejudice which colours their whole lecture. Others are for some reason or another emotionally involved in the subject of their lecture. In both cases, these lecturers may consciously – or subconsciously – mask several of the important points they intend to make. It is possible, therefore, that recognition of the salient points of a lecture is made more difficult by the attitude of the speaker. Because of his particular attitude or standpoint, the speaker may be led into highlighting what is subsidiary – or even irrelevant – to the main point of a part of his lecture.

   Spkr's attitude can make recogntn of key pnts diffclt.

2 Most students have good intentions about studying. Indeed, we can even make the same remark about teachers and lecturers: I have met very few people who dislike work or who set out with the intention of doing as little work as possible. And yet, as with students, somehow relatively few teachers achieve the goals they set for themselves. Quite simply, they do not succeed in doing the work they have planned to do. We have seen that initial inertia destroys many good intentions of students: 'Tomorrow is the day when the lazy man works.' For student and lecturer alike, it is all too easy to waste time even after having embarked on a task. Friends call; you feel tired; or you have an important letter to write. Whatever the reason, you break your routine of study. This is why a timetable is so necessary. Without it to guide you, it is difficult to plan and keep to any regular routine of study. I have heard so many excuses for failure to reach a short-term or long-term goal, but the reason in every case is simply a failure to keep to a timetable of study.

   Timetable = nec to establish study periods.

C Reading: Skills involved in note-taking

Read the following text as fast as you can in order to obtain a general idea of the content. The maximum time allowed for each section is $1\frac{1}{2}$ minutes.

Skills involved in note-taking

Section 1

Note-taking consists of various complex sub-skills. In order to take notes effectively during a lecture, it is necessary to be familiar not only with the grammar, vocabulary and phonological features of the language but also with the particular conceptual and rhetorical features employed. The student must be able to comprehend the argument, select the main points and follow the way in which they are developed. Although these principles apply equally to taking notes from books, we shall concentrate first on taking notes in lectures, since this particular skill generally constitutes a major source of difficulty for the foreign learner.

The extent of the student's familiarity with the subject of the lecture and the background knowledge at his disposal are clearly of enormous help in enabling him to determine the salient points of the lecture. Emphasis is conveyed by a speaker's particular treatment of his subject: that is, by the length of time he devotes to certain topics, the manner in which he develops his ideas and the extent to which he makes use of such features as repetition. Emphasis, however, may also be conveyed in several other ways. Some lecturers vary the pace of their delivery, slowing down to indicate an important point. Others speak more loudly or more deliberately in order to indicate what is important. Intonation features (ie the rise and fall of the voice) are also used to denote something important. Indeed, even pauses and slight changes in breathing are used subconsciously in lectures by native-speakers to indicate intentions and attitudes. Furthermore, such cues are by no means confined to verbal delivery: they are shown by gesture (especially by the use of the hands), by body movements, and, perhaps most important, by the eyes. All these elements vary from language to language and must be taken into account.

True/False

Now write T if each statement is true according to the writer and F if it is false or untrue.

1 It is necessary to master many language skills in order to take good notes.
2 A previous knowledge of the subject often makes it more difficult to select the important points of a lecture.
3 Emphasis is denoted by the way a lecturer treats a particular subject, by the way he speaks and by the gestures he uses.
4 The way in which a speaker pauses may show his attitude or his intention.
5 Gestures – the use of the eyes, the hands and the body – are helpful for the foreign learner because they have the same basic meaning in all languages.

Instead of

Look carefully again at the text in order to complete the following statements. Give the actual words the writer uses.

6 Instead of saying that students must have a good knowledge of the sentence patterns, words and sounds of a language in order to take notes in that language, the writer says that they _____

7 Instead of saying that a student's knowledge of the subject will be useful for him to recognise the main parts of the lecture, the writer says that this knowledge will be _____

8 Instead of saying that certain lecturers change the speed at which they speak during a lecture, the writer says _____

9 Instead of talking about the rise and fall of the voice, the writer uses the phrase _____

10 Instead of saying that the way in which intentions and attitudes are shown is not linked solely to speech, the writer says that _____

Section 2

Subtle signalling devices (usually referred to as markers) are used in lectures to indicate intentions and attitudes. Such devices are important in enabling the listener to follow a line of thought and to recognise the salient features of a lecture. Since these signalling devices usually operate at a fairly deep, subconscious level among the native speakers of a language, it is difficult to isolate them for learning purposes. Indeed, it would be misleading to attempt to construct a comprehensive list of particular words and phrases which can act as signalling devices. The following examples are given merely to indicate how markers may be used in particular contexts to signal various intentions and attitudes. The purpose for which each of the markers is used in its context is indicated in brackets.

1 *What I want to do now is to show*
  Let me first show } how systematic methods of study can be of
  I'm now going to talk about
  positive help in enabling students to achieve long-term goals. (Introducing a particular subject and informing the audience of the speaker's intention.)

2 Many students frequently fail to reach their objectives. *Have you ever wondered why this is so? Why* are their aspirations ahead of their actual progress? (An attempt to obtain the participation of the audience.)

3 Research has shown that the average student retains very little of the information given in a lecture.
  In fact, } it was found that as little as 15% of the information given in a lecture
  Indeed,
  was retained longer than a day. (Denoting repetition or a rewrite of a particular point – generally for the sake of emphasis.)

4 *You might be tempted to think* } lectures are intended primarily to stimulate the
  It's all very well thinking that
  student. (Signals that the speaker is anticipating the views of his audience and intends to correct or contradict them.)

5 *Let me repeat*
 I want to emphasise
 The point I'm making is } that merely writing out fair copies of one's notes is a
 What's significant is

waste of valuable time. A critical review of the notes taken, however, is a different matter. (Signals denoting emphasis.)

True/False
Now write T if each statement is true according to the writer and F if it is false or untrue.

11 The signalling devices the writer mentions are often called markers.
12 It is possible to isolate and to learn most of the signalling devices used to indicate intentions and attitudes in a lecture.
13 Native speakers are usually not consciously aware of the many subtle signalling devices which are used in a lecture.
14 The writer cites the phrases *In fact* and *Indeed* as examples of restating something for the sake of emphasis.
15 It is advisable for students to draw up long lists of examples of signalling devices.

Instead of
Look carefully again at the text in order to complete the following statements. Give the actual words the writer uses.

16 Instead of saying that signalling devices help the student to follow an argument, the writer says that _____ .
17 Instead of using the word *separate* when talking about the difficulty of learning signalling devices, the writer uses the word _____ .
18 Instead of saying that it would be harmful to give a long list of words and phrases for signalling intentions and attitudes, the writer says that _____
19 Instead of saying that the second example shows the speaker is trying to gain the active interest of his listeners in his lecture, the writer says that the speaker is making _____
20 Instead of saying that *Let me repeat* shows the speaker wishes to stress the importance of a particular point, the writer says that these words are _____

Section 3
An ability to perceive relationships between different ideas, states, actions and processes is essential in note-taking. Economy is of the utmost importance in notes, and thus it is highly advantageous to substitute a sign or symbol for the words expressing a relationship between two ideas. In addition to the speed with which it can be produced, a particular sign can often be used for a number of different words or phrases. For example, a similar kind of relationship is expressed by *because, as, for, since, as a consequence of*, and *resulting from*. If we are able to recognise the basic

relationship implicit in all these words and to use the symbol '∴' to denote this relationship, we can save valuable time and produce accurate notes. The various symbols used to denote such relationships will be introduced gradually throughout this book. The following are given below now, however, as examples of a few of the common signs which can be used in notes:

1	=	is, equals, is the same as, is like, is equivalent to, is synonymous with, may be regarded as, consists of, is made up of, is called, represents, is on a par with
2	→	leads to, causes, results in, becomes, moves towards, passes into, makes, is converted into, is formed into
3	↗	grows, increases, rises, climbs, improves, helps; more, greater, increasing, rising; growth, increase, improvement
4	∴	therefore, thus, so, then, consequently, with the result that, so that
5	⊃	if, on condition that, provided that, so long as, supposing

True/False
Now write T if each statement is true according to the writer and F if it is false or untrue.

21 It is useful to include in notes signs to show relationships.
22 One sign or symbol (eg ∴) can be used to replace a number of different words.
23 It is generally unnecessary to identify the basic relationships implied in these symbols.
24 The sign ↗ means *with the result that*.
25 The words *if* and *so long as* can be shown by the same symbol.

Instead of
Look carefully again at the text in order to complete the following statements. Give the actual words the writer uses.

26 Instead of saying that it is important to be able to recognise connections between different ideas, the writer says that _____
27 Instead of saying that it is important to write notes as briefly and as quickly as possible, the writer says that _____
28 Instead of saying it is very useful to replace words with signs or symbols, the writer says that _____
29 Instead of referring to fundamental connections between words like *because, as, for, since,* etc, the writer refers to _____
30 Instead of recommending the use of *leads to, causes, results in, becomes,* etc in notes, the writer recommends the use of the following symbol: _____.

Section 4
Other features of note-taking involving the omission of words, abbreviations and

word compression have already been dealt with. However, if the student meets anything unfamiliar in a lecture, he is advised to take down word for word as much as he can and to check with his colleagues or with the lecturer as soon as possible afterwards. Indeed, any point on which there is even the slightest degree of misunderstanding or confusion should be discussed with the lecturer.

It is advisable to put each main idea in the form of a heading in the notes. Each point should then be numbered and written near the left-hand margin of the paper. All subheadings should be given another number or letter: eg if Arabic numbers (1, 2, 3, etc) are used for main headings, then either lower case letters (a, b, c, etc) or small Roman numerals (i, ii, iii, etc) should be used for the various subheadings. In addition, the subheadings should be indented: ie they should start half an inch or so to the right of the main headings. Information conveyed under these subheadings is easily read if indented by a further half-inch. Since there is no one universal system in operation, it is necessary for the student to devise the particular method which he finds suits him best. Here is an example of outline notes of the previous talk given for listening practice. (For an explanation of the symbols used, please see pages 57, 58, 64 and 65.)

General Principles of Note-Taking

1. Note-taking
     i) ↗ recall
     ii) ⟶ active particptn ∴ ↗concentrtn.

2. Amount of notes
        Varies with type of lecture.
        Also own knowl helps.

3. 3 approaches to n-t.
     i) Full notes BUT repttn and not distinguish btwn imp and unimp points. Also no time to digest lecture.
     ii) No notes BUT memory = unreliable.
     iii) Outline notes
          ∴ must dist between imp and unimp and see reltnship btwn ideas.
             Diff btwn notes from book and lecture
                 glance thru first   pict grad emerges
                          | |
                 outline ⟶ detail   detail ⟶ outline

4. Review notes soon after lecture ∴ fresh in mind.
       Not copy out notes BUT read thru crit and amplify.

5. Take notes in Eng.
       Transl = hard but odd words in own lang = useful.

Most of what has been written about note-taking in lectures applies to taking notes from books. However, since it is possible in this case to gain a rough idea of the framework of the written material before any notes are taken and since it is possible to refer back or forward in the text, note-taking from books usually presents less of a problem for the foreign learner. Not only can the relationships between the various ideas in the text be noted at leisure but the identification of the key sentence in a paragraph will make it much easier to note any salient point. Hence, intelligent underlining of points in the text or circling of key phrases, though perhaps not as useful as outline notes, has certain merits if the student is fortunate enough to own the book which he is using. It should go without saying that critical comments written in the margins have even greater merit.

True/False
Now write T if each statement is true according to the writer and F if it is false or untrue.
31 When a student h :ars a completely unfamiliar phrase in a lecture, he should not attempt to include it in his notes.
32 It is very useful to number headings in notes and to indent wherever possible.
33 It is easier to take notes when reading a text than when listening to a lecture.
34 Students should not be encouraged to underline points in a text.
35 It is useful to write comments at the side of the reading text.

Instead of
Look carefully again at the text in order to complete the following statements. Give the actual words the writer uses.
36 Instead of saying that the student should write each word of something unfamiliar in a lecture, the writer says that _____
37 Instead of saying that it is advisable to write subheadings to the right of the main headings, the writer says that _____
38 Instead of saying that there exists no single method which everyone uses, the writer says that _____
39 Instead of saying that taking notes of lectures is similar in many ways to taking notes of books, the writer says that _____
40 Instead of talking about how different points in the text are connected with one another, the writer uses the phrase _____

Note-taking practice
Now reread the compl :te text carefully and make notes.

NOTES
Skills involved in Note-taking
1. Note-taking = complex sub-skills
        i) gr, vocab, etc.
        ii) select main points, etc.

2. Identfctn of main points
    i) Knowl of subj helps.
    ii) Emphasis shown by treatment of subj [time,
       manner, etc.] place, intontn, pauses, gesture.

3. Signalling devices [i.e. markers]
    Indicate intentions and attitudes.
    V imp but operate at subconsc level.
    E.g. = In fact/Indeed – signal rewrite [us for emphasis].

4. Relationships
    1 sign = diff words/phrases
        e.g. ∵ because, as, for, resulting from, etc.

5. Other features = omission of words, abbrevtns, compression.
   If something unfam – copy down and check later.

6. Lay-out : i) Headings = main ideas [1, 2, 3].
        ii) Number points [a,b,c] or [i, ii, iii].
        iii) Indent.

7. N-t from books : i) Same but easier because
          a) idea of framework first
          b) refer back/forward
          c) see rltnships at leisure
          d) identfcn of key sentences helps.
        ii) Underlining key words = useful but
         crit comments better.

Writing practice

Use the notes to write an account of the difficulties and the skills involved in taking notes during lectures. Finish your account by writing a few comments on suitable ways of setting out notes and by providing *an example of your own.*

D Practice section

For each of the following five paragraphs, write not more than one line of notes.

1 Many students always carry with them a large number of exercise books, carefully selecting the appropriate one for each lecture. Others carry with them just one thick exercise book, transferring their notes at the end of each day or week to the appropriate notebook. All these students have completely overlooked the advantages of possessing a loose-leaf notebook. Every lecture – no matter what the subject is – can be recorded in a loose-leaf notebook. Later each lecture can be transferred to its appropriate place in a similar file kept at home. A pack of plain

white cards can be used on the same principle as the loose-leaf file. I know of one person who carries around a wooden box full of white cards. But this is very bulky and not nearly so convenient as a loose-leaf file.

2 It is often difficult to interpret and record a lecturer's attitude towards his subject. Avoid further confusion resulting from trying to 'correct' it while you are taking notes and from writing down your own attitude or your own reactions. It is always advisable to remain neutral while taking notes of a lecture. Never attempt to write down what you think the speaker should have said. Write down only what he has actually stated. If you want to query a particular point, put a cross or a question mark in the margin. In this way you will be able to show your disagreement or desire to consider later at greater length the particular point which has been made.

3 A large number of students make neat copies of their notes at the end of each day. They write them out neatly or type them before putting them away in the appropriate file. Considerable time and effort is expended on making these neat copies. Indeed, the whole process often takes up several hours of study time each week. This is quite clearly a waste of valuable time. It is far better to write your notes reasonably neatly while you are actually making them in the lecture. As soon as possible afterwards, you can then read critically through the notes and make comments. Ask yourself questions and do some supplementary reading. If you think it helpful, set yourself a short written assignment. But don't waste time on simply copying out the notes neatly.

4 So far we have not mentioned the matter of finding a suitable place for studying. Clearly, any student who is determined enough can study anywhere – in a crowded room, on a bus, in his bedroom, and so on. Many students, in fact, vary their place of study from day to day, complaining that they soon become tired and restless if returning to the same place for more than a day or two. But this method of changing one's place of study is not as sensible as it may at first seem. It is now generally agreed by psychologists and study specialists that one set place for study is preferable to moving about. It is good for the student to learn to associate one particular place with study. Such an association can, by itself, be conducive to establishing good study habits and a desire to study. The place selected for study, moreover, should be reasonably quiet and free from distractions. Although certain people boast that they can even study in front of a television set, it is doubtful if anyone can work really effectively amongst distractions of this nature.

5 You should make yourself comfortable when you are studying, but you should guard against relaxing too much. The amount of work you can do sprawled in an armchair may not be great. Some students argue that they can study just as well in bed as in a library, but lying down is by far from an ideal position for studying. The best position for most students is to sit upright – preferably at a table. An ordinary wooden chair is best suited for this purpose. An upright position gives you a sense of alertness and purpose. You are far less likely to fall asleep in such a

position than if you were lying down on a bed or a sofa. Moreover, your attention will not be inclined to wander in the same way it would if you were sprawled in an armchair.

Unit Four
Improving your reading

A Listening comprehension: Increasing reading speed

Listen carefully to the talk which you are about to hear. Answer each question below *when you are instructed to do so.*

Increasing reading speed

1 Complete the following sentence according to what has been said. (Write several words to replace each blank.)

Two main factors in helping to increase reading speed are _____ and

_____ .

2 Choose the best answer, *a, b* or *c*:

The phrase *transfer of training* from one language to another is used in this context to refer to

   a the effect of reading improvement techniques on learning to speak a foreign language.

   b the relation between speed reading in the foreign language and reading with comprehension in the mother tongue.

   c the possibility of reading techniques in the first language improving reading in English.

3 According to what you have just heard, write T if the following statement is true and F if it is false:

Reading quickly is useful if we want to find out how important a certain text is for our purposes.

4 Complete the following sentence by writing one word to replace each blank:

The following example shows the recognition or v_____ s_____ of a certain reader.

The eyes / fixate / on a / point / and / take in / letters / or words / on either / side / before / moving on / to the / next point. /

5 According to what you have just heard, write T if the following statement is true and F if it is false:

The following exercises are very useful for increasing the speed of reading a text:

a   Read each line as quickly as possible. Underline all the words that are the same as those on the left.

1 float	flood	float	floor	fleet	flow
2 exist	exit	excite	exist	exhile	exist
3 require	inquire	request	require	inquest	acquire
4 forget	forgot	forgive	forge	forget	forego

b   Look at the vertical line and run your eyes down it, reading the words in each column.

red	sky
full	moon
warm	night
small	river
shallow	stream
deserted	seashore
beautiful	countryside

6 Complete the following sentence according to what has been said. (Write several words.)

The method which the speaker recommends to increase reading speed is to _____

B Note-taking: Synonyms, word compression and omission of examples

The note-taking skills can be further developed by practice in the following methods of reducing and summarising the original material: 1 the use of synonyms for long words, 2 word compression, and 3 the omission of examples, repetition, etc. (All the examples of these features have been taken from the tapescript of the talks in this unit.)

1   *The use of synonyms for long words:* Instead of long words or phrases in your outline notes, much shorter synonyms can often be used: eg *usually* instead of *almost invariably, can* instead of *are quite capable of, hard to ensure* instead of *difficult to make sure of.* As with the use of abbreviations, this method of reducing the amount of writing necessary saves time and enables the listener to concentrate on digesting what is being said in the talk or lecture.

2   *Word compression:* There are many ways of compressing word groups: for example, the following adnominal phrases can be compressed without difficulty:
the speed of reading = reading speed
the same form of script = same script (form)

It is impossible to compile any comprehensive list of rules in a short space: only familiarity and practice in using English will help you to realise that sentences like:

A typical length of time our eyes stop is one-tenth of a second.

can be compressed to:

Our eyes stop for one-tenth of a second.   (Sentence)
= Eyes stop 1/10 sec.   (Equivalent in notes)

and statements like:

There are numerous exercises designed to increase our span of recognition.

can be reduced to:

Many exs to increase recogntn span.

Note, however, that if the meaning or implication of a phrase is not fully understood, it is advisable to write down the whole phrase (using the original words) so that it can be studied and digested later.

3 *Examples, repetition, etc:* When taking notes, the student should be wary about noting down information which is being repeated, even if in a slightly different way. Such repetition is often used in talks and in lectures as a way of emphasising or clarifying certain points. Irrelevant information, often given in the form of digressions, should also be avoided in notes. Examples frequently come under this category, although it is generally possible to reduce an example to a word or a short phrase. Since it is not difficult to remember an example (especially in the form of an anecdote or quotation involving personal experience), one or two words will usually be adequate. In the short lecture in this unit on *Increasing reading comprehension* listen for the example referring to 'thade' and simply write out this word in your notes.

C Lecture: Increasing reading comprehension

Extract

A *Reference*

In written language certain words refer either 1 'backwards' to words or information that was given earlier or 2 'forwards' to words or further information that is to follow. The reader must be able to identify reference features from clause to clause and sentence to sentence.

1 One method of continuing reference is by
   a   the repetition of the topic noun phrase
       There is at present a danger of too great a concern with *reading speeds*. *Reading speeds* are meaningless unless accompanied by comprehension.
   b   repetition with an expanded noun phrase
       One of the most difficult language tasks confronting many students at university is *note-taking*. *Taking outline notes of lectures* demands a number of important skills.

   c the use of a related noun

So far little has been said about study during the *vacations. Holidays* present an ideal opportunity for supplementing study.

2 Backward reference to a topic is also denoted by

  a the use of a substitute noun (or noun phrase):

one, the one(s), some, the same, the former . . . the latter, both, all, several, etc.

Some students take no notes, trying to listen critically to the lecture. Other students, however, take detailed notes, hoping to digest them after the lecture. *The former* rely completely on their memory while *the latter* rely on their ability to interpret their notes.

  b the use of pronouns:

     i   personal (particularly *he, him, she, her, it, they, them*)

    ii possessive

   iii demonstrative

   iv relative

    v reflexive

Most students who take detailed notes have little time to reflect on the ideas being communicated. *They* fail to see the general for a mass of detail.

  c the use of *(no) such, a similar one* to refer back to modifiers:

Many students think that there is a foolproof method to increase their vocabulary range within a few hours: they discover too late that there is *no such* method.

  d the use of *do* + (it), (so), (too), (the same) as predicate substitutes:

John enjoys studying English; most of his friends *do, too.*

  e the use of the complement substitute *so* after *think/expect/believe/be/ gather/guess*, etc:

Helen thinks good study methods are essential: I *think so*, too.

  f the use of *the* in the second mention of the noun phrase:

A poor reader may use a ruler to help him to read: he will probably hold *the* ruler under each line he reads.

B *Linkage*

Phrases, clauses and sentences are joined by appropriate linkers. An ability to recognise important linkers or connectives will greatly assist in the comprehension of a text. The following list contains examples of linking devices.

1 Linkers of addition:

  a within a sentence: and, both . . . and

                       not only . . . but also

                       as well

                       either

Detailed timetables $\left\{\begin{array}{l} and \\ and\ also \\ as\ well\ as \\ together\ with \end{array}\right\}$ short-term objectives

are of immense help in forming a study routine.

b   linking sentences: Also, And, Moreover,
                         In addition, Furthermore,
                         Likewise, Again, Neither

Note-taking is important as an aid to recall.

$\left.\begin{array}{l} In\ addition, \\ Moreover, \\ Furthermore, \end{array}\right\}$ it provides a means by which the student

can participate actively in the lecture.

2 Linkers denoting alternatives:

a   within a sentence: or, either . . . or
        The student may prefer to do his most difficult work *either* late at
        night *or* early in the morning. Rarely will he want to do it in the
        afternoon.

b   linking sentences: Either, Alternatively, Otherwise
        The student may take very detailed notes during lectures. *Alternatively,*
        he may take none at all, relying entirely on his memory.

3 Linkers denoting contrast:

a   within a sentence: But, Yet, While, Whereas, Although, (Even) though,
                         Despite, In spite of

$\left.\begin{array}{l} Although \\ Even\ though \\ While \end{array}\right\}$ certain people move their lips when reading,

some of them still manage to read fairly quickly.

b   linking sentences: Nevertheless, However, Again, On the one hand . . .
                         on the other (hand)

        On the one hand fast reading is important; *on the other hand* certain
        texts require to be read slowly and carefully.

4 Linkers showing a time relationship:

                    When, At the same time (as), Whenever, Every time,
                    The moment, Immediately, (Just) as soon as, Since, After,
                    Before, Until, Once

$\left.\begin{array}{l} Whenever \\ When \\ As\ soon\ as \\ The\ moment \\ Once \end{array}\right\}$ you begin to feel tired or bored,

take a short break from your studying.

5 Linkers indicating conditions : (Even) if, If (only), Unless, As long as,
In the event of, Given (that), Provided (that)

If
Provided that
As long as   } appropriate study methods are used, students should
Given that
Granted

have little difficulty in following a course of advanced study.

6 Linkers denoting purpose: in order to, in order that, to, so as to, so that,
with the intention of

It is useful to file your notes systematically {
  to
  in order to
  so as to
  so that you can
}

find them easily for revision purposes.

7 Linkers denoting cause: because, since, as, as a result of, owing to the fact that
Students should try to take outline notes in a critical way

because
since
as   } many lectures contain a lot of redundant
owing to the fact that
information.

8 Linkers indicating result:

 a   within a sentence: so (that), with the result that
Take notes neatly *so that* you will not have to waste time copying them
out again.

 b   linking sentences: Therefore, Thus, Consequently

The average student finds he has a great deal of reading. {
  Consequently
  Therefore,
  Thus,
}

it is very important for him to develop effective reading strategies.

9 Linkers denoting exception: except (for), except (that), with the exception of,
excepting, apart (from), not counting, excluding

Many students begin to change the entire routine of their private lives

except for
with the exception of   } their sleeping habits.
apart from

(Based on a paper by B E Foster: *Some of the skills required for writing well-formed English prose.*)

NOTES

Increasing Reading Comprehension

1. Comprhnsion = v imp
   See words w eyes; select inf w brains.
   Ntve spkr knows grammar. So can select and read fast.

2. Reference devices
   Can refer back or fwds: e.g. pronouns
                                    the former...the latter

3. Linkage [linkers/connectives]
   Imp signposts : e.g. addition a) in sentence
                                     and, not only.... but also
                                  b) link sntncs
                                     Moreover, In addition

4. Vocabulary
   i) Dictionary interrupts reading.
      Bad because time spent.
   ii) Deduce meaning fr context: e.g. thade [tutorials].
   iii) Relate word to others: synonyms and antonyms.

5. Reading prac = v imp
   If book = diffclt read. Then read easier bk for fun.

Writing practice
Use the notes together with appropriate examples from the extract preceding them to write a brief account of the function of reference devices and connectives in English prose.

D Practice section

1 The following exercise provides practice in the use of connectives and reference. Rewrite the passage, selecting the most appropriate word or group of words from those given in the brackets.

The importance of a varied and flexible approach to reading cannot be too greatly stressed. (*So as to/For to/In order to*) achieve (*this/the/much*) flexibility, (*it/there/one*) is often necessary to aim at increasing reading speed. (*So/Such/ That*) an aim, (*although/despite/however*), should never mask the importance of comprehension in reading. (*Indeed/In addition/Otherwise*), the most important factor in reading is not speed but efficiency: that is, the ability to derive the maximum benefit from reading without any wastage of time and effort.

On the one hand, (*therefore/so/thus*), (*it/this/he*) is unwise to place too great an emphasis on speed to the detriment of comprehension. (*On the other hand/On the contrary/On the opposite side*), an effort to increase reading speed should be made at the outset. For certain purposes, (*he/it/one*) is far better to read at a speed of 300 words per minute with a fair level of comprehension than at a speed of 100 words per minute with near-perfect comprehension. (*Nevertheless/Likewise/Consequently*), anyone reading with full comprehension is probably not reading as quickly as (*he/one/it*) is capable of (*being/doing/having*). In any case, (*since/when/for*) written prose contains a large element of redundancy, much of the important information conveyed in a text is generally repeated in one form or (*two/other/so*).

2 Deduce the meanings of the words in italics from the contexts in which they appear.

   a After reading the following extract, draw a picture of a *denorm*.

   'When I entered the room, I saw an old man sitting at a desk. He was gazing almost horizontally at a large book supported on a denorm. As I moved forwards, he pressed a tiny button at the bottom of the denorm. The arm of the denorm shot out and turned over the page of the book. I looked carefully at the title of the book, printed in large letters on the back of the book and just visible through the open framework of the denorm. The book was called *Notorious Poisoners*. The old man quickly sensed that I was looking at the title and suddenly switched off the denorm light.'

   b The following two brief extracts have been taken from C A Mace's *The Psychology of Study** and illustrate how this principle of deducing the meaning of words works in actual practice.

      i 'The neglect to answer a letter may be the cause of much distraction. The rankling of an insult to which we failed on the spur of the moment to find an apt retort may spoil a morning's work. . . . We may write the neglected letter, or purge ourselves of passion by a walk, and a little concentrated thought upon the matter that disturbs us.'
      An insult is said to *rankle* when:
      A the cause of it is unknown or puzzles a person
      B it amuses a person and makes him laugh
      C a person is irritated and annoyed by it

      ii 'In vacations a timetable is a matter for self-directed study. It is a useful way of dealing with initial inertia and for circumventing distractions.'
      When we *circumvent* distractions, we _____

*C A Mace *The Psychology of Study*. Penguin, 1968.

Unit Five
Lectures

A Listening comprehension: Listening to lectures

Listen carefully to the talk you are about to hear. Answer each question *when you are instructed to do so.*

Listening to lectures

1 According to what you have just heard, write T if the following statement is true or F if it is false:

The speaker thinks that the chief function of the lecture is to convey information.

2 Complete the following sentence by writing one word to replace each blank:

Important points in a lecture can be easily identified *a* if the student is _____ with the subject of the lecture and *b* if he is aware of the various s_____ d_____.

3 Write one word to replace the blank in *a* and several words to replace the blank in *b*:

a During a lecture you should try to think _____.

b You can prepare for lectures by doing some preliminary reading. How else can you prepare for them?

By _____

4 Choose the best answer, *a, b* or *c*:

As soon as possible after a lecture you should

a relax in a free period.

b study a book for the next lecture.

c read through your notes.

5 Complete the following sentences by writing one word to replace each blank:

Even _____ native _____ miss certain _____, they _____ still understand the _____. However, many _____ learners need every _____ to understand each _____.

6 Write T if the following statement is true or F if it is false:

The speaker feels it is important for students not to miss lectures.

B Note-taking: Signalling devices (1)

Examples of ways of signalling intentions and attitudes were given in the reading text
in Unit 3. An awareness of such devices is of great use in identifying important points
and ideas in a talk or lecture. Although neither the following list nor that given in
Unit 6 is intended to be comprehensive in any way at all, it provides a simple
illustration of the kinds of 'markers' or verbal clues which can signal an important
point in a lecture.

Introduction of an important point

1 A speaker may state his intention to introduce a new or an important point in any
 of the following ways:
 What I would like to do now is _____
 I want to start by trying to _____
 The subject/topic/idea/point I intend to discuss/deal with/explain/examine/
 concentrate on is _____

2 The speaker may even attempt to justify the introduction of an important point:
 There are several reasons/causes for examining _____
                         means/ways of looking at _____

3 He may wish to introduce a point by asking a (rhetorical) question:
 Have you ever thought/wondered/considered why/how _____ ?
 Is it reasonable to assume that _____ ?
 Why should _____ ? How does _____ ?

Dealing with the main point or emphasising a point

1 The speaker may pause, reduce the pace of his delivery, or vary his intonation to
 indicate that he is making an important point:
 The point is _____ The thing _____
 The question I want to ask is _____
 The point I am making is _____
 It would seem to me that _____
 It strikes me that _____
 This is important/significant because _____
 Basically _____ Fundamentally _____

2 The speaker may wish to repeat the point for emphasis or state it in a different
 way:
 Let me repeat/stress that _____
 That is to say _____
 So what we now have is _____
 In fact _____ In other words _____

Drawing conclusions from important points

Some speakers may regard the conclusions to be drawn as more important than the original idea itself. Other speakers may draw conclusions almost as an afterthought. Their attitude to the conclusions they draw may be established more by the manner of delivery of this part of the lecture than by the following clues:

Therefore, _____ Consequently, _____

As a result, _____

Because this is the case, _____

This being true/the case, _____

If this is so/true, then _____

If we accept this, _____

C Reading: What can the lecture achieve?

Read the following text as fast as you can in order to obtain a general idea of the content. The maximum time allowed for the first section is 2 minutes and for the second section 3 minutes.

What can the lecture achieve?

Section 1

There has been much recent criticism of the lecture as an effective method of teaching. In a report on university teaching methods by the Hale Committee (1964) the lecture was found to be less popular with students than other methods of teaching. The title of a recent book by D A Bligh *What's the Use of Lectures?* reflects the current attitude towards lectures (even though the book itself attempts to provide information about the lecture method by presenting an analysis of the techniques likely to make the lecture effective). In spite of its apparent unpopularity, however, the lecture still continues to be the main instrument for teaching in higher education.

What are some of the arguments against the lecture? Firstly, if the chief function of the lecture is inspirational, then 90% of lectures would appear to fail miserably. Tutorials are far more effective in stimulating an interest in the subject. Again, if its chief purpose is to provide information, then this can be far better done by books and by handouts. Indeed, a large amount of detailed information in a lecture has been found to act as a barrier against learning.

Another criticism is concerned with the lack of training of most university lecturers. Few lecturers in Britain, for instance, have ever received any professional training in lecturing or teaching. Some academics openly scorn teaching and proudly claim to be the world's worst teachers. Even many of the more enlightened lecturers tend to regard teaching as an interruption in their real work, namely research.

Consequently, it is hardly surprising that in some recent research studies students appear to be opposed more to current lecturing techniques than to the lecture itself. Indeed, many attacks on the lecture are really attacks on ineffective lecturing techniques. If the lecture is to achieve anything, therefore, the first requirement is an improvement in lecturing techniques. Lecturing is of little use unless communication takes place and good conditions for learning are created. The lecturer must first prepare his lectures carefully, and thought must be given not only to content and originality of approach but also to presentation and delivery. Would shorter lectures prove more efficient, leaving time for questions and discussion? Could more consideration be given to the differing standards of the students in the audience? How useful would supplementary notes be? Could the lecturing technique be combined with any other method? What scope is there for blackboard diagrams and charts? Could slides or film be used to provide immediacy or the illusion of reality? When planning the lecture, the lecturer should consider all these aspects, examining carefully the various types of teaching techniques which he could use as an integral part of his lecture.

True/False

Now write T if each statement is true according to the writer and F if it is false or untrue.

1 The Hale Committee's investigation concerning university teaching methods found that the lecture was as popular with students as most other methods of teaching.
2 Most lectures do not stimulate students into wanting to learn more.
3 The lecture is best at providing a lot of detailed information.
4 Several lecturers in Britain proudly claim that they have little teaching ability.
5 Most students seem to complain more about the lecturing methods used than of the place of lectures themselves in a university.
6 It is generally advisable not to attempt to combine the lecturing technique with other teaching methods.

Instead of

Look carefully again at the text in order to complete the following statements. Give the actual words the writer uses.

7 Instead of saying that *What's the Use of Lectures?* shows us what students think of lectures, the writer says that the book _____
8 Instead of saying that lectures still form the most important part of teaching at colleges and universities, the writer says that _____
9 Instead of saying that lectures are not as good as tutorials in making students interested in the subject, the writer says that _____
10 Instead of saying that the ability to teach is looked down upon in universities, the writer says that _____
11 Instead of saying that students seem to dislike the ways in which lectures are given rather than the lecture itself, the writer says that _____
12 Instead of saying that the lecturer should study all the ways in which he can present his material in a lecture, the writer says that _____

Section 2

Insofar as it is subject-centred instead of being student-centred, the approach to learning in higher education is different to that in schools. Rarely does the lecturer take into account the capacity of his students to conceptualise: he is more concerned with the concepts themselves. Nevertheless, the lecture is a far better place to convey new and difficult concepts than the textbook. Furthermore, although the inspirational function of the lecture is scorned by some critics, the lecturer can be highly successful in conveying a feel for his subject, especially when he is completely at home with the concepts, the facts, and the skills he is teaching. It is precisely in this way that the lecture can increase motivation.

Motivation also results simply from attending a lecture with one's fellow-students. If the whole group focuses attention on one particular subject at the same time, an atmosphere is created which is highly conducive to learning. Group discussion can then be much more meaningful, since all members of the group have undergone the same experience and reached the same stage in their approach to the subject. In this way every student will have a clearer sense of direction.

The lecture has another advantage insofar as it can present the student with an up-to-date picture of the most recent developments in a particular field. No book can do this half so well as the lecture. Indeed, many books written for advanced courses are out of date by the time they are published; even the various scholarly papers and journals date rapidly nowadays. In the lecture, however, all this new knowledge is unfolded against a background of earlier knowledge with which the lecturer is usually extremely familiar.

The lecture also offers an excellent means of guiding the student through the many routes in his particular subject. Many lectures are of necessity eclectic, but they prevent the student from losing himself in a mass of reading.

It may be argued, however, that a good tutorial can do almost everything that a lecture does. This is by no means true. Many topics require a careful and an uninterrupted treatment – which only a lecture can give. The ideas are understood much more easily if conveyed in a continuous, unbroken sequence, especially in the case of certain complex theories and the working out of difficult formulae. The use of blackboard diagrams to show how the various steps in a certain process are built up may form an invaluable part of the lecture.

Provided that the purpose of the lecture is carefully considered, the lecture plays an important role in teaching. Although it may not be suited to all aspects of learning, it can do many things extremely well, particularly if the lecturer has had a sound training in the various techniques of lecturing and is able to combine his approach with other appropriate teaching techniques.

True/False
Now write T if the statement is true according to the writer and F if it is false or untrue.

13 The 'feel' for a particular subject cannot be conveyed successfully in a lecture.

14 Attending a lecture in a group with one's fellow-students is an advantage in itself.

15 Very few specialist books and papers are out-of-date by the time they are published.

16 Lectures can lead the student through a mass of reading material, thus saving him valuable study time.

17 It is better to convey ideas on many topics in a continuous sequence without interruption.

18 The writer doubts the value of lectures in higher education.

Instead of
Look carefully again at the text in order to complete the following statements. Give the actual words the writer uses.

19 Instead of saying that universities concentrate more on the subject itself than on the individual student in their teaching, the writer says that _____

20 Instead of talking about the ability of students to understand abstract notions and ideas, the writer talks about _____

21 Instead of saying that the lecture can inspire students and make them familiar with a subject, the writer says that it can _____

22 Instead of saying that a group of students can feel they want to learn after attending a lecture, the writer says that _____

23 Instead of saying that in many lectures information has to be selected from various sources, the writer says that _____

24 Instead of saying that certain ideas are communicated better if there are no interruptions, the writer says that they _____

Note-taking practice
Now reread the complete text carefully and make notes.

NOTES

What Can the Lecture Achieve?

1. Crit of lecture
            e.g.   i) Hale Report on univ t methods – Lecture = less
                      pop than other mthds.
                  ii) 'What's the use of lectures?' [Bligh] – title.
                      [BUT book analyses effctve techniques]

2. Against Lecture
                  i) If insp function – 90% fail.
                 ii) If give inform – better in books.
                iii) Little profssnl training – poor teaching.

3. Students opposed to L techniques but not L itself.
Lctrs must improve techniques: eg combine with
other methods?
standards, notes,
diagrams, slides?

4. For lecture
i) Th L is subj-centred and not stdnt-centred, conveys feel for subj.
ii) Motivtn because in group.
iii) Gives up-to-date inf. [Books - not.]
iv) Guides stdnts.
v) Often nec to give ideas in unbroken order.

5. Lecture is imp if purpose understood
esp if i) L has training
ii) combines other t techniques.

Writing practice

'The lecture is of little use as an instrument for teaching and ought to be abolished.'
Use the notes above to refute this argument.

D Practice section

Complete the following questionnaire about the last lecture you attended:

1 *Information*

   i How much information was transmitted in the lecture?

     a A lot   *b* A medium   *c* Only a little   *d* None
                        amount

   ii How many sources did the lecturer draw on?

     a A lot   *b* A medium   *c* Only a few   *d* None
                        number

   iii How useful was the lecture in providing a guide to the background reading, etc?

     a Very useful *b* Useful   *c* Only a little   *d* Not useful
                                useful

   iv How difficult did you find the subject?

     a Very   *b* Difficult   *c* Fairly difficult   *d* Not difficult
        difficult

  v How original do you think the lecture was?
      a Very   *b* Original   *c* Fairly original   *d* Unoriginal
          original

  vi How much did you learn from the lecture?
      a A lot   *b* A medium   *c* Only a little   *d* Nothing
               amount

2 *Organisation*
  i Did you feel the lecture progressed according to a plan? Yes/No

  ii How did the lecturer introduce the particular topic of his lecture?

  iii How frequently did the lecturer digress?
      a Frequently *b* Fairly   *c* Only rarely   *d* Not at all
                   frequently

  iv What provision was made for questions? (Comment on this aspect of the lecture and refer to any questions which you asked or remember.)

  v What supplementary material was used?
    Film/Slides/Tapes/Diagrams/Demonstrations/Handouts

  vi Comment on how this was used. (In the case of handouts, state whether these complemented the lecture or were simply duplicated notes of the lecture.)

3 *Delivery*
  i Was the lecturer audible? Yes/No/Sometimes

  ii Did he make any special allowance for the foreign learners of English (eg through repetition, diagrams, use of blackboard, etc)? Comment.

  iii Where did you sit in the lecture room?

4 *Effect of lecture*
  i To what degree did it make you think?
      a A lot   *b* A medium   *c* Only a little   *d* Not at all
               amount

  ii What questions did it raise (after the lecture)?

  iii Did it increase your interest in the subject? Yes/No

  iv If yes, in what way?

  v Did it succeed in changing any of your previous attitudes to the subject? Yes/No

  vi If yes, in what way?

5 *Additional comments*

Using the questionnaire as a guide, write detailed comments on the next lecture you attend.

Unit Six
Using a dictionary

A Listening comprehension: What kind of dictionary?

Listen carefully to the talk which you are about to hear. Answer each question below *when you are instructed to do so*.

What kind of dictionary?

1 According to what you have just heard, write T if each statement is true or F if it is false.
   a A good dictionary prescribes rules about which words to use.
   b Most dictionaries do not include regional variations of language.
   c Dictionaries often become out of date because the language of a community is always changing.
2 Complete the following sentence according to what you have just heard. (Write several words.)
   The Italian word *simpatico* and the English word *privacy* are mentioned as examples of _____
3 Choose the best answer, *a, b* or *c*:
   Dictionaries specially written for the foreign learner are useful because:
   a they contain derivations of words.
   b they are written in a controlled vocabulary.
   c specialised words needed in one's studies are included.

B Note-taking: Signalling devices (2)

This section shows further ways of the use of verbal clues to indicate important points and new ideas. Remember, however, that the lists give *examples* of the kind of clues to be aware of and they should not be learnt by heart. Such an emphasis on the particular words and phrases listed here would only result in the student missing other vital clues in a talk or lecture.

Moving from one idea to another

Any well constructed lecture will progress gradually and systematically from one
point to another. 'Markers' may take the following forms:

The next question is _____
There is another consideration, and this is _____
Furthermore, _____
Next/Then/Secondly/Subsequently/Finally _____
Having established/seen/examined/found that _____, let us now _____
It is now time to/necessary to _____
If these facts are true, then _____

Contrasting ideas

The speaker may wish to contrast ideas or to balance one point against another:

On the one hand, _____   On the other hand, _____
However, _____   Nevertheless, _____   Although _____
In contrast to _____

Disagreeing with points

Sometimes the speaker may advance one idea only to contradict it later, thereby
forestalling potential criticism of the main point he wishes to emphasise. Speakers
generally use such an approach to show their audience that they have carefully
considered both sides of an argument.

You might be tempted to think that _____
It's all very well saying that _____
Some experts argue that _____ but _____
It has been said (in the past) that _____ but _____
It's all very well to _____ but _____
On the face of it _____   Superficially _____

C Lecture: What a dictionary contains

The following extracts (1A & B) provide examples of how pronunciation and stress
can be denoted in dictionaries and reference works. Most of the symbols commonly
used in phonetic transcription in dictionaries are drawn from the alphabet authorised
by the International Phonetic Association. However, since a few of the symbols
adopted are sometimes given different values by phoneticians, students should
become familiar with both the consonant and vowel values in the notation contained
in the particular dictionary which they are using. Phonetic symbols are given in
Extract 1A while diacritical marks are shown in Extract 1B. Again it should be noted
that the different kinds of diacritical marks are often used in different dictionaries.

Extract 1

A

Key to Pronunciation and Stress

I. Pronunciation

A. Vowels and Diphthongs

Symbol	Examples	
æ	cat [kæt]	man [mæn]
ɑː	father ['fɑːðə]	part [pɑːt]
ɔ	on [ɔn]	hot [hɔt]
ɔː	saw [sɔː]	port [pɔːt]
ou	go [gou]	road [roud]
ɔi	point [pɔint]	boy [bɔi]
ai	fly [flai]	fright [frait]
au	out [aut]	now [nau]
e	get [get]	men [men]
iː	me [miː]	see [siː]
ei	eight [eit]	day [dei]
əː	herd [həːd]	first [fəːst]
i	it [it]	sing [siŋ]
ə	above [ə'bʌv]	rubber ['rʌbə]
iə	near [niə]	here [hiə]
ɛə	share [ʃɛə]	hair [hɛə]
u	full [ful]	put [put]
uː	too [tuː]	fool [fuːl]
ʌ	up [ʌp]	come [kʌm]
uə	tour [tuə]	poor [puə]
ɔə	four [fɔə]	more [mɔə]

Note: *Four* and *more* may be pronounced [fɔː] and [mɔː].

B. Consonants

The following symbols have their customary English sounds:

[b d f h k l m n p r v w z]

Symbol	Examples	
k	cap [kæp]	kick [kik]
g	gap [gæp]	big [big]
tʃ	chin [tʃin]	each [iːtʃ]
dʒ	jam [dʒæm]	judge [dʒʌdʒ]
ŋ	long [lɔŋ]	bring [briŋ]
s	sack [sæk]	ice [ais]
ʃ	ship [ʃip]	mission ['miʃən]
ʒ	measure ['meʒə]	revision [ri'viʒən]
θ	thin [θin]	mouth [mauθ]
ð	this [ðis]	heather ['heðə]
j	yes [jes]	yacht [jɔt]

Notes

1. A symbol in italic type denotes that the sound it stands for is often not pronounced by many speakers, especially in rapid speech: secondary ['sekəndəri].

From the *Overseas Students' Companion to English Studies* by J B Heaton and J P Stocks. Longman.

B
COMPLETE PRONUNCIATION KEY

The pronunciation of each word is shown just after the word, in this way: **ab·bre·vi·ate** (ə·brē′vi·āt). The letters and signs used are pronounced as in the words below. The mark ′ is placed after a syllable with primary or strong accent, as in the example above. The mark ′ after a syllable shows a secondary or lighter accent, as in **ab·bre·vi·a·tion** (ə·brē′vi·ā′shən).

Some words, taken from foreign languages, are spoken with sounds that otherwise do not occur in English. Symbols for these sounds are given at the end of the table as "Foreign Sounds."

a	hat, cap	i	it, pin	s	say, yes
ā	age, face	ī	ice, five	sh	she, rush
ä	care, air			t	tell, it
ä	father, far	j	jam, enjoy	th	thin, both
		k	kind, seek	th	then, smooth
		l	land, coal		
b	bad, rob	m	me, am		
ch	child, much	n	no, in	u	cup, son
d	did, red	ng	long, bring	u̇	put, book
				ü	rule, move
e	let, best	o	hot, rock	ū	use, music
ē	equal, see	ō	open, go		
ėr	term, learn	ô	order, all		
		oi	oil, toy	v	very, save
		ou	out, now	w	will, woman
f	fat, if			y	you, yet
g	go, bag	p	pet, cup	z	zero, breeze
h	he, how	r	run, try	zh	measure, seizure

ə occurs only in unaccented syllables and represents the sound of *a* in *a*bout, *e* in tak*e*n, *i* in penc*i*l, *o* in lem*o*n, and *u* in circ*u*s.

FOREIGN SOUNDS

Y as in French *lune*, German *süss*. Pronounce ē as in *equal* with the lips rounded for ü as in *rule*.

œ as in French *deux*, German *könig*. Pronounce ā as in *age* with the lips rounded for ō as in *open*.

N as in French *bon*. The N is not pronounced, but shows that the vowel before it is nasalized.

H as in German *ach*, Scottish *loch*. Pronounce k without closing the breath passage.

From *The Thorndike-Barnhart Comprehensive Desk Dictionary*. Doubleday, New York.

Extract 2

Examples of how four dictionaries deal with the word 'study'.

> **study** (8-1) to work at a subject in order to learn it; subject to be learnt; rough drawing or painting, or unfinished piece of music; reading- and writing-room of one person; *In a brown study* = deep in thought and not noticing those around.

From the *New Method English Dictionary*. Longman.

study[1] /ˈstʌdɪ/ n (pl -dies) **1** [U and in pl] devotion of time and thought to getting knowledge of, close examination of, a subject, esp from books: *fond of* ∼*: give all one's leisure time to* ∼*; make a* ∼ *of the country's foreign trade. My studies show that....* **2** [C] sth that attracts investigation; that which is (to be) investigated; *humane studies. The proper* ∼ *of mankind is man. His face was a* ∼, was well worth observing closely. **3** *be in a brown* ∼, musing, unaware of people, happenings, etc near one. **4** room used by sb (e g in his home) for reading, writing, etc: *You will find Mr Green in the/his* ∼. **5** sketch etc made for practice or experiment; piece of music played as a technical exercise. **6** [U] (old use) earnest effort: *Her constant* ∼ *was how to please her husband.*

study[2] /ˈstʌdɪ/ vt,vi (pt,pp -died) **1** [VP6A,8, 15A,2A,B,4A] give time and attention to learning or discovering sth: ∼ *medicine. He was* ∼*ing for the medical profession/*∼*ing to be a doctor.* **2** [VP6A] examine carefully: ∼ *the map.* **3** [VP6A, 4A] give care and consideration to: ∼ *the wishes of one's friends/only one's own interests.* **4** (pp) **studied**, intentional, deliberate: *a studied insult.*

From the *Advanced Learner's Dictionary of Current English.* Oxford University Press.

stŭd′y̆[1], n. **1.** Thing to be secured by pains or attention (*it shall be my* ∼ *to please, to write correctly; your comfort was my* ∼ *; make a* ∼ *of,* try to secure). **2.** (Now usu. *brown* ∼) fit of musing, reverie, (*there he stood for an hour in a* ∼ *; is in a brown* ∼, too intent on his thoughts to observe what is passing). **3.** Devotion of time & thought to acquiring information esp. from books (often pl.), pursuit of some branch of knowledge, (*gives his hours to* ∼ *; make a* ∼ *of,* investigate carefully ; *my studies have convinced me that; the* ∼ *of* *mathematics, morals* ; *continue your studies,* go on with your lessons). **4.** Thing that is or deserves to be investigated (*the proper ~ of mankind is man* ; *his face was a ~*). **5.** (Paint. etc.) sketch made for practice in technique or as preliminary experiment for picture or part of it (*his studies are exquisite, but his finished work disappointing* ; *a ~ of a head*); (mus.) composition designed to develop skill in some particular branch of execution; (theatr.) *good, slow,* etc., learner of parts (UNDERSTUDY). **6.** Room used for literary occupation, transaction of business, etc. (*you will find him in his, the, ~*). [ME *studie,* f. AF & OF *estudie* f. L *studium* zeal, study]

stŭd′y̆[2], v.t. & i. **1.** Make a study of, take pains to investigate or acquire knowledge of (subject) or to assure (result sought), scrutinize or earnestly contemplate (visible object), (*~ law, French, philosophy* ; *~ book,* read it attentively ; *~ one's part,* try to learn it by heart ; *~ up,* get up for examination etc. ; *~ out,* succeed in finding out by hard thinking ; *studies others' convenience, his own interests* ; *~ person's face* or *character, a map, the stars*). **2.** Apply oneself to study esp. reading (*~ for the bar,* read law). **3.** (arch.). Meditate, muse. **4.** Be on the watch, try constantly to manage, *to* do (*studies to avoid disagreeable topics*). **5.** p.p. Deliberate, intentional, affected, (*a studied insult* ; *with studied politeness, rudeness, unconcern, abandon*), whence **stŭd′iedLY**[2] (-dĭd-) adv. [ME *studie,* f. OF *estudier* f. med. L *studiare* f. L as prec.]

¹study \'stədē, -di\ *n* -ES [ME *studie*, fr. OF *studie, estudie* state of perplexity or reverie, application of the mind to the acquirement of knowledge, study, fr. L *studium* eagerness, application of the mind to the acquirement of knowledge, study; akin to L *studēre* to be eager, be diligent, study and prob. to L *tundere* to beat — more at STINT] **1** : a state of absorbed contemplation, perplexity, or reverie : ABSTRACTION ⟨paused and appeared to be in a deep ∼ —Alexander MacDonald⟩ ⟨the long silences that meant I was lost in ∼ —Eve Langley⟩ **2 a** : the application of the mental faculties to the acquisition of knowledge ⟨is in your own power greatly to improve . . . by ∼, observation, and reflection —Earl of Chesterfield⟩ ⟨hours of ∼ and careful thought —Bruce Payne⟩ ⟨years of ∼ in school and college⟩ **b** : such application of the mind in a particular field or to a specific subject matter ⟨scholarship . . . which illuminates the ∼ of the family —Lynn White⟩ ⟨taking up the ∼ of history⟩ ⟨enter upon the ∼ of law⟩ **c** (1) : a careful examination or analysis of a phenomenon, development, or question usu. within a limited area of investigation ⟨plunged into the ∼ of latex —Clarence Woodbury⟩ ⟨*studies* have been made of individual cases and of groups of adolescents —H.R. Douglass⟩ — often used with *under* ⟨further reductions are under ∼ —D.D.Eisenhower⟩ (2) : a paper or monograph in which such a study is published ⟨these two volumes constitute the ablest ∼ on the iron and steel industry —*Current Biog.*⟩ ⟨publishes *studies* and reports⟩ **3 a** : a building or room furnished esp. with books and devoted to study or literary pursuits ⟨set out my typewriter in the ∼ . . . to write —Worth T. Hedden⟩ **b** *obs* : the books contained in such a study or in a collection **c** *obs* : a place of learning : UNIVERSITY, STUDIUM GENERALE **d** : the lower level of the inner stage of an Elizabethan playhouse often used to represent an indoor scene **4 a** *obs* : an expressed inclination : DESIRE, INTEREST **b** : a consciously reasoned effort : PURPOSE, ENDEAVOR ⟨those favors which it will ever by my ∼ to deserve —W.S.Gilbert & A.S.Sullivan⟩ ⟨it has been the ∼ of my life to avoid those weaknesses —Jane Austen⟩ **5 a** : an organized branch or department of learning : SUBJECT ⟨what are your favorite *studies* —G.B.Shaw⟩ ⟨was . . . on the faculty of graduate *studies* —Edna Yost⟩ **b** : the activity or work of a student ⟨the curriculum for graduate ∼ —E.B.Nyquist⟩ ⟨returning to his *studies* after vacation⟩ **c** : something that is the object of one's study ⟨was pompous and wonderfully conceited, his every word and every gesture a careful ∼ —Marcia Davenport⟩ ⟨about the use of making this sugar . . . I said I made it my ∼ —H.D.Thoreau⟩ **d** : something attracting close attention or examination usu. by reason of contrast or conflict ⟨it was quite a ∼ to watch the faces round the table — in the struggle between good manners and amusement —Rachel Henning⟩ ⟨a ∼ in conflicting emotions —T.B.Costain⟩ ⟨the whole show a ∼ in tolerant condescension —David Driscoll⟩ **6** : one who memorizes something (as a part in a play) — usu. used with a qualifying adjective ⟨is not considered a fast ∼, but once he has learned a role he has it for good —H.C.Schonberg⟩ **7 a** : an artistic production in any of the fine arts intended as a preliminary outline or esp. as an experimental expression or interpretation of specific features or characteristics ⟨a number of his drawings were *studies* of beggars, clowns, cripples, and street musicians —*Current Biog.*⟩ ⟨a ∼ in tunes, all of them beautiful and separate —Leonard Bernstein⟩ ⟨whether dancing in dramatic roles . . . or *studies* in pure dance —*Current Biog.*⟩ **b** : a literary work serving as an experimental or esp. as an exploratory analysis or portrayal of carefully observed features of character or motivation ⟨a particularly successful ∼ of the type of grievance-ridden, unhappy . . . misfit —R.P.Fleming⟩ ⟨a topical ∼ of life in a wartime services canteen —Leslie Rees⟩ ⟨a brilliantly intuitive ∼ of war and the emotions of men in combat —*Time*⟩ **8** : a musical composition usu. devoted entirely to a special problem of instrumental technique : ÉTUDE

²**study** \"\ *vb* -ED/-ING/-ES [ME *studien*, fr. OF *estudier*, fr.
ML *studiare*, fr. L *studium*, n., study] *vi* **1 a :** to apply the
mind to the acquirement of knowledge through reading and
reflection, observation, or experiment ⟨he might have
studied through the literature to the mind of that century
—T.S.Eliot⟩ **b :** to undertake formal study of a subject or
course ⟨*studied* at Manual Arts high school —Lillian de
Tagle⟩ ⟨*studied* with the faculty of law at the university —
Current Biog.⟩ ⟨*studied* under him at the university —*Current
Biog.*⟩ **2** *dial* **a :** to consider deeply **:** MEDITATE, REFLECT —
usu. used with *about* ⟨looking at the oil in the bottle and smell-
ing it and tasting it, and ~*ing* about what it meant —H.H.
Martin⟩ **b :** to deliberate something with oneself **:** DEBATE ⟨stood
digging a bare big toe into the dirt and *studied* awhile —F.B.Gip-
son⟩ — usu. used with *on* or *about* ⟨I'm ~*ing* on whether I ought
to sell —Jean Stafford⟩ **3 :** to consider something as one's aim
: ENDEAVOR ⟨I *studied* to appear calm…so as to draw him on to say
more —W.H.Hudson †1922⟩ ⟨appears to ~ to repress these
things in his poetry —David Daiches⟩ ~ *vt* **1 a :** to read (a
book or writing) in close detail often with the intent of learning
for recall ⟨was set to ~*ing* the Talmud for 15-hour stretches —
Current Biog.⟩ ⟨stopped and *studied* a big sign in front of a
large store —Irving Bacheller⟩ **b :** to learn (as a part) for
playing ⟨you could . . . ~ a speech of some dozen or 16 lines —
Shak.⟩ ⟨waiting in the wings ~*ing* his part⟩ **2 a :** to apply the
mind to the learning or understanding of (an area of knowledge) ⟨learns a good deal by simply ~*ing* human nature⟩
⟨*studies* the advances in his profession every free moment⟩
b : to occupy oneself with the formal study of (a subject,
course, or activity) ⟨planning to ~ medicine⟩ ⟨*studies* the
violin at the conservatory⟩ ⟨attends night school to ~ typing⟩
c : to do special reading about for a specific purpose — usu.
used with *up* ⟨thought I knew something . . . because I'd
studied it up in a book —Calder Willingham⟩ **3 :** to make a
plan for **:** PLOT, DESIGN ⟨he *studies* our overthrow and generally
seeks our destruction —Robert Burton⟩ — usu. used with *out*
⟨works hard ~*ing* out a new system⟩ **4 a :** to observe or
analyze in detail (a phenomenon, development, or question)
usu. within a restricted area with a view to some action **:** IN-
VESTIGATE ⟨experts ~ tides and ocean currents —H.M.
Parshley⟩ ⟨~*ing* the mood of people in different quarters —
Evelyn G. Cruickshanks⟩ ⟨~*ing* and attempting to solve the
economic problem —*Current Biog.*⟩ **b :** to examine closely to
understand or determine something ⟨each still ~*ing* the other
with interest —Agnes S. Turnbull⟩ ⟨the brakeman . . . took
advantage of each curve to ~ the train —*Monsanto Mag.*⟩
⟨*studied* the flames as if seeking the answer . . . in their restive
pattern —Walter O'Meara⟩ **5 :** to employ thought and careful attention in ⟨the epistle . . . was *studied* and recopied and
elaborated —Anthony Trollope⟩ **6 :** to pay heed to or be
solicitous for (a person's feelings or convenience) ⟨needed a
home and a wife who would ~ his comfort —Edith Sitwell⟩
syn see CONSIDER
³**study** \'stədi, -tùdi\ *Scot & dial Eng var of* STITHY

NOTES

<u>What a Dictionary Contains</u>
1. Alphabet order of words [1st letter, 2nd, 3rd, etc.]
   Guide words — top of page.
2. Inf given in dictnry:
         i) Spelling — inconsistncs in Eng, so don't guess.
        ii) Syllable divsn.
              Useful for [a] end of line splitting and [b] pronun.
       iii) Pronun
              Shown by [a] phon symbols or [b] diacrit marks.
              Phon s are more diffclt but more exact
                                    also used by many dicts.
        iv) Pts of speech — e.g. 'couple' is n + v.
              Adv. Learner's shows count/uncount.
         v) Meanings
              Shows first either [a] most common meaning
                                or [b] earliest mng.
              Meaning depends on context.
        vi) Sp uses of wds
              [a] lit   [b] archaic   [c] colloq   [d] slang

Writing practice

Using the notes above, write a brief account of the type of information contained in
the *Advanced Learner's Dictionary* (or any other good dictionary). Choose examples
from the dictionary to illustrate each point.

D Practice section

1 Write out the following words in alphabetical order:
     liability, legislate, likely, limit, liberty, like, liable, level, lexicon, library,
     life, legal, legion, leopard, lighten, lesson, leprosy, likelihood, limit,
     literature
2 Write down the symbol used in your dictionary for each of the vowel sounds
   in italics:
     f*a*ther, c*a*t, *a*te, p*e*n, w*a*ter, im*a*ge, gl*a*ss, gl*u*cose, gond*o*la, g*o*lden, har*a*ss,
     h*a*tred, hist*o*ry, h*o*pe, b*u*tter, *o*nly, *o*riginal, pr*e*clude, pr*e*vious
3 There are only THREE different vowel sounds in all the words in the following
   list. Make three columns and write each word in the appropriate column (ie
   according to its vowel sound).
     hot, saw, go, caught, or, prompt, walk, want, spoke, wrought, stole, fork,
     mock, wart, malt, hall, mosque, moat, what, sprawl

4 Use a dictionary to mark the syllable carrying the primary or main stress in each of the following words:

recollection, subject (v), familiarise, distribute, interpret, originality, pedestal, questionnaire, frequent (v), debatable, provocative, guarantee

5 The following words are connected with study. Use your dictionary to write down for each word *a* the pronunciation, *b* the part(s) of speech, and *c* the meaning:

motivation, thesis, distraction, schedule, efficient, etymology, fixate, vocalisation, glossary, regression, lexicography, peripheral

6 In Unit 7 you will read about *skimming* techniques. As suitable preparation, therefore, several meanings of the verb *skim* are given below. They are presented in the same way as a dictionary would show them.

1 remove from the surface of a liquid   **2** clear a liquid of something floating on the surface   **3** move lightly over   **4** make something go lightly over   **5** glide or fly (rapidly) along   **6** cover with a thin layer of   **7** deal superficially with something   **8** read hastily or quickly, read only the important points.

Which of the meanings listed above do you think *skimming* in Unit 7 will have? Now number each of the following sentences according to the appropriate meaning of the verb *skim*:

a   Several birds skimmed by as we were talking.

b   Poor Tom fell down and went skimming over the ice.

c   The whole path was skimmed with a slimy green substance.

d   Dr Brown skimmed over several important aspects of conservation in his lecture.

e   Skim the milk before you drink it.

f   If you skim through Chapter 8, you will get a clear picture of the author's point of view.

g   The old lady skimmed the oil off the wine and put a large glass in front of me.

h   Can you skim such a large stone across the river?

Unit Seven
Reading textbooks

A Listening comprehension: Skimming

Listen carefully to the talk which you are about to hear. Answer each question below *when you are instructed to do so.*

Skimming

1 Complete the following sentences according to what has been said. (Write several words to replace the blanks.)
   a When we read normally our eyes concentrate on _____ but when we skim our eyes become aware of _____
   b Although the eye movements appear to move in no regular direction, they are influenced by _____ and _____

2 According to what you have just heard, write T if the following statement is true and F if it is false:
   We should try to maintain the same level of comprehension when we are skimming as when we are reading.

3 Complete the following sentence according to what has been said:
   The application of skimming techniques enables us to find out whether a book will be _____

4 Complete the following sentences by writing one word to replace each blank:
   a We scan when we want to locate _____ information.
   b After finding the information we want, it will probably be necessary for us to read the appropriate section _____.

5 *a* Give another name for selective reading.
   b When is this technique used?

6 According to what you have just heard, write T if the following statement is true and F if it is false:
   Only those students who can read quickly can learn how to skim successfully.

B Note-taking: Relationships (1)

As was demonstrated in the reading text in Unit 3, the ability to recognise basic relationships is essential for successful note-taking. Although sets of relationships are expressed by numerous verbal equivalents, the basis of each set can often be shown by a single visual symbol. An awareness of fundamental relationships between words and ideas is thus one of the most important aims in seeking to attain the required skills of note-taking. Consequently, each section in Units 7–10 will concentrate on giving examples of the various symbols commonly used in notes. (The lists of verbal equivalents given for each sign are far from being exhaustive: in most cases only a limited selection of verbal equivalents is given.)

1   =   is, equals, is the same as, is like, is synonymous with, consists of, is made up of, is called, represents, is on a par with

> There are some reading texts which are packed with information.
> Some texts = full of inf.
> Words which denote linkage are called linkers or connectives.
> Words showing linkage = linkers/connectives.
> Signs represent relationships between various words and ideas.
> Signs = reltnships btwn words and ideas.

2   ≃   (is) approximately, (is) more or less

> The reading speed of many foreign learners of English at university is approximately 150 words per minute.
> Many f-leaners' r speed ≃ 150 wpm.
> or
> Many f-leaners read at ≃ 150 wpm.

3   /   not

> This symbol is used to reverse the polarity of a relationship:
> eg ≠ means *is not, does not equal, is different from*
> Many exercises designed to train the eye are not very useful.
> Many exs for training eye ≠ useful.
> The Italian word 'simpatico' does not mean the same as the English word 'sympathetic'.
> Simpatico (It) ≠ sympathetic (Eng).

4 important   quite, rather, fairly (important)

    important   very, considerably (important)

    important   very, extremely   (important)

> Underlining is used in notes to show various degrees of importance or emphasis.
> The ability to read quickly is very important.
> Able read quickly = imp.
> A timetable is an extremely effective means of helping the student to establish and maintain a routine of study.

Timetable = <u>effective</u> in est study routine.

5   ∴   therefore, thus, so, then, consequently;
with the result that, as a result, so (that)

Reading requires the ability to understand the relationship between words. Consequently, for these reasons, many experts have now begun to question the usefulness of eye training.

Reading = und reltnship btwn words ∴ eye training ≠ useful.

Many native language-to-English dictionaries contain numerous errors and so should be avoided by the student.

Many Ll-Eng dictnrs = many errors ∴ avoid.

6   ∵   because (of), as, since, for, as a result of, on account of, owing to, due to, now that

A considerable number of speed reading courses are successful since students attending them want to read quickly and are prepared to practise a lot.

Many speed rdng courses = success ∵ stdnts i) want to improve and ii) practise hard.

Almost all dictionaries give guide words at the top of each page: these guide words, often printed in heavy type, can save the reader a great deal of time in locating a particular word.

Can find words quickly ∵ guide words in most dictnrs.

C Reading: The SQ3R method

Skim through the following text in order to obtain a general idea of the SQ3R method. The maximum time allowed is 90 seconds.

The SQ3R method

That aspect of reading with which students are most concerned is the study of textbooks. Although studying a textbook encompasses reading, it involves much more than reading. This is demonstrated clearly by what is probably the most popular technique* for dealing with textbooks. This technique, commonly referred to as the SQ3R method, is described in detail here and is strongly recommended for studying an important text, the contents of which you need to know thoroughly. It consists of the following five steps:

*S*urvey
*Q*uestion
*R*ead
*R*ecall
*R*evise (or *R*eview)

*Based on the method developed by F P Robinson and described in *Effective Study*. Harper and Row, 1946.

1 *Survey.* Look through the whole of the textbook before studying the various parts in detail. Glancing through the material very rapidly will help to establish a familiarity with the plan and organisation of the book. It will throw light on the aims and the method the author uses to achieve these aims. First, a scrutiny of the title page of the book will provide basic information on the topic of the book. Even the author's name and the date of publication may be of direct relevance. The Preface, Foreword, or Introduction to the book will state the author's aim and describe the various features of the book. It will generally inform you of the audience for whom the book is intended and of the kind of information contained in the book. After skimming through this section, turn next to the Table of Contents for information on the topics contained in the book. This is generally the quickest and the easiest way of determining what the book is about. From the Table of Contents you may be able to see how topics are related to one another and into which broad divisions they fall. Sampling the Index (ie finding out the main references) is also a useful practice when surveying the book. An index provides a more detailed presentation of the topics listed in the Contents section, but does not show the relationship between the topics. If the book is considered useful for your requirements, a rapid survey of the individual chapters will now be necessary. When conducting such a survey, glance at the beginning and the end of each chapter as well as at the various section headings and end-of-chapter summaries (if any). A cursory glance at any glossary and bibliography will complete the survey stage.

2 *Question.* The next stage in the process necessitates the formulation of questions and imparts a sense of direction and purpose to the reading. You will probably ask general questions after surveying the book as a whole. For example, what do you need to know? What do you already know? What do you expect to learn from the book? How can you break up the book into sections for study purposes? How can you approach the book? A survey of each individual chapter of the book will then produce more specific questions. The introductory sentences in each chapter and section of the book are of great help in the formulation of specific questions. Occasionally, the author may set out by deliberately posing questions. If headings are used, simply transform each heading into the interrogative, for specific questions will lead to the adoption of an active approach to reading. Always write out your questions either in full or in note-form, dealing with one section or one chapter at a time.

3 *Reading.* The next step is to read the book as quickly as possible, but not in the same way as you would read a novel. Indeed, habits arising from reading novels may be harmful when applied to reading textbooks. The reading of a textbook will often of necessity be slower. Frequent regressions may occur, and you may find yourself turning back pages in an effort·to understand more clearly the various relationships treated or the arguments developed. The questions formulated in the previous stage should now be answered during the reading, every attempt

being made to approach the book actively. It is not too late to formulate any questions omitted previously and to check them against your preliminary survey and questions. Although many reading specialists would advocate the taking of notes in the next stage, it is possible at this stage to take useful notes from a reasonable unit of text (eg from a section or a chapter). Remember, however, that it is better not to make notes while you are actually going along: try to make them after finishing reading part of the section.

4 *Recall.* At the end of each section or chapter, attempt to recall the contents. Read out your original questions and attempt to provide an answer to each question. If a friend or colleague has read the same material, you can formulate questions to ask each other and to discuss. The more frequent the opportunity for recall, the stronger the material will be fixed in your mind. The recall stage is the time to check and amplify your notes – or, if you have not already done so, to make notes. This stage is generally considered to be the most active of the five stages in the SQ3R method, requiring more time to complete than any other stage.

5 *Revise.* Revision shortly after the previous steps have been completed is useful in ensuring that the information learnt is retained for a longer time. One method of revision recommended is to look again critically at the material as a whole, writing a form of summary or discussing it comprehensively. Some students prefer to read another textbook on the same topic, checking the new information against the notes they have made and, where necessary, expanding the original notes. Another form of revision recommended for later purposes (ie before an examination) takes the form of a very rapid repetition of the previous four steps in the SQ3R method. Clearly, after the four steps have been completed once, your revision will take only a fraction of the time spent in the first instance.

In conclusion, the SQ3R method is recommended as a means of generating an active participation in study and an intelligent attitude towards the material being studied. It is preferable by far to the widespread habit of opening a book and reading through it page by page, since it ensures a much higher degree of both comprehension and retention.

Pause and think carefully about what you have read. Now list the various steps in the SQ3R method and write at least one sentence about each of the steps.

Note-taking practice
After completing the first exercise, check each statement with the text and take outline notes.

NOTES
The SQ3R Method
     SQ3R method = ~~pop~~
1. Survey
     i) Title page gives basic inf on topic.

ii) Preface, Fwrd, Intro give aim and pass outline.

iii) Table of Contents shows reltn of topics to each other.

iv) Index gives detailed list of topics.

v) Survey of chapters — skim.

vi) Glossary and bibliography.

2. Question

Gen qstns from book: specific ones from chs.

Intro sntnces lead to qstns. [Headings, etc.]

Qstns encourage active approach.

3. Reading

Read quickly [but ≠ novel: e.g. regressions nec].

Answer qstns now and ask others.

Take notes at end of sctn or ch.

4. Recall

= Try to remember reading.

Read orig qstns — answer. Discuss.

More opp for recall = better remember.

Check or make notes.

Most active stage in SQ3R.

5. Revise

Revise soon ∴ remember more.

Rvsn =   i) review material and write summary

+/or   ii) read other text bk on same subj

+/or   iii) repttn of 4 steps [quick].

Writing practice

Using the information in the notes above, describe the SQ3R method, illustrating how you would use it by referring to a textbook which you have recently read.

D Practice section

1 Apply the SQ3R method to this book.

  a Survey: i   Make a note of the title, author and date of publication.

          ii   Summarise in one or two sentences the main points in the Introduction.

          iii   Table of Contents: Which of the following topics occupy complete chapters in the book?

              Memory/Research/Dictionaries/Skimming/

              Organisation of study/Note-taking/Reading speed/

Lectures/Topic sentences/Vocabulary/Libraries/
Timetables/Study skills and objectives/Tutorials/
Reading textbooks/Health/Writing reports/
Reading improvement/Abbreviations/
Examinations/Reference techniques/Studying in
English

iv Each unit in the book is divided into 4 sections. Name
each of these sections.

b Question: i Write down one or two general questions about the book
as a whole and one or two questions about some of the
specific topics it contains.

ii Now write down a few questions arising from a survey of
the first reading text in Unit 1.

c Read: i Read the text in Unit 1.

ii Answer the questions you formulated in the previous
stage.

iii Now answer the questions on the whole book.

d Recall: Make outline notes of the first six chapters.

e Revise: After three days, survey the book once more, repeating
steps *a–d*.

2 Imagine that you are writing a book review for a local university/college/school
journal. Write a brief summary of this book, outlining its contents and
commenting on those parts which you think will prove useful and on those which
will not be so useful.

Unit Eight
Learning in small groups: Tutorials and seminars

A Listening comprehension: Improving your speaking ability

Listen carefully to the talk which you are about to hear. Answer each question below *when you are instructed to do so.*

Improving your speaking ability

1 Complete the following sentence according to what you have just heard. (Write several words.)

It is possible to improve speaking ability on a self-study basis but _____

2 Write T if each of the following statements is true or F if it is false according to what you have just heard:

  a Films and TV programmes are a fairly useful means of helping you to improve your ability to speak.

  b Accurate imitation is much more difficult than many students realise.

  c It is better to work through several pronunciation exercises fairly quickly rather than to work through only one exercise carefully but slowly.

3 Write one word to replace the following blank:

In order to distinguish between sounds when speaking, you must first be able to _____ the difference between them.

4 Complete the following sentence by writing one word to replace each blank:

Stress consists of _____ stress and _____ stress.

5 How is correct and natural intonation achieved? (Write a sentence.)

6 Choose the best answer, *a*, *b* or *c*

After the early stages of learning pronunciation, the foreign learner of English should concentrate on

  a perfect pronunciation.

  b successful communication.

  c accurate sentence structure.

B Note-taking: Relationships (2)

Note that the first two signs in this section can be used as verbs, adjectives, adverbs and occasionally as nouns. However, with all the signs listed in this section, care should be taken to avoid ambiguity in notes. (For example ↗ reading can be achieved if _____ Does ↗ denote *better, more* or *faster*?)

1   ↗   grows, increases, becomes larger, rises, climbs, improves;
        more, greater, increasing, rising;
        growth, increase, improvement
>   The ability to skim properly will increase the flexibility of your whole approach to reading.
>   Skimming ↗ flexibility of reading.
>   Although most foreign learners of English at colleges and universities are primarily concerned with improving their ability to read and write English, many also want to speak English more fluently.
>   Most students want to read and write Eng ↗, but many also want speak ↗.

2   ↘   decreases, reduces, lessens, shrinks, becomes less/fewer, drops, falls, deteriorates, sinks, goes down, lowers;
        less, fewer, weaker, decreasing, reducing;
        decrease, reduction, decline, deterioration, depreciation
>   Skimming may reduce general comprehension to 50% as compared with 80% or 90% comprehension gained from ordinary reading.
>   Skimming ↘ gen comprehension (50% cf 80–90% in ord reading).
>   Regression results in a marked decrease in reading speed.
>   Regression ↘ reading speed.

3   ↑   high, tall, deep, vast, great, much, a lot of, big, large;
        height, depth, vastness, enormity
>   The ability to identify the main ideas in a text is of great importance in skimming.
>   Identfctn of main ideas = ↑ imp in skimming.
>   or   Identfctn of main ideas = imp in skimming.

4   ↓   low, shallow, small, few, scarce, tiny, minute;
        scarcity, smallness, lack
>   Many students fall behind in their studies because of a lack of effective reading techniques.
>   Many ↘ in studies ∵ ↓ good reading methods.

5   ↥   the highest, the tallest, the deepest, the greatest, the most
>   Many study specialists argue that fluent reading is the most important of all the study skills.
>   Many spclsts say fluent rdng = ↥ imp study skill.

6   ↧   the lowest, the smallest, the least, the scarcest, the tiniest

Reading aloud is the least useful of all the language skills practised
in the higher forms of the secondary school.

Reading aloud = $\downarrow$ useful skill in upper sec school.

7   →   leads to, causes, results in, becomes, moves towards, passes into,
makes, is converted into, is formed into

Progress on a self-study basis may be slow and difficult, but intelligent
and systematic practice can lead to an improvement of the oral skills.

$\nearrow$ on self-study basis = diffclt but systmtc practice → $\nearrow$ oral skills.

Native language-to-English dictionaries encourage the tendency to
regard each new item in English as having a one-word equivalent in
the student's mother tongue.

Ll-Eng dictnrs → think each Eng word has equiv in Ll.

8   ←   comes from, results from, develops from, is a result of, is caused by,
is produced from, is made from, is based on

After the initial stages, your ability to talk English can be developed
only by frequent practice in conversation and discussion.

After 1st stages oral ability $\nearrow$ ← practice in converstn.

English usage is determined by the people who use the language –
not by any language academy.

Eng usage ← by spkrs of lang $\not\leftarrow$ by lang academy.

C Lecture: Tutorials and seminars

NOTES

Tutorials and Seminars

1. Confsn re t & S.

    T = small group — assignments; tutor = authority

    S =   "   "   — works at adv level — sp aspects – Q & A.

2. Informal disc group

    Spontns but ↑ potentials if

      i) l stdnt = well-informed

      ii) disc = not too unformal

      iii) prep reading.

3. Stdnt = silent if

      i) lacks confid in Eng

      ii) nothing to say.

    ∴ Prepare topic and want to talk.

4. Not worry re mistakes [n-spkrs → mistakes]

    Commnctn of ideas = better than correctness.

When statement = approp → stdnt = encouraged
correct form = reinforced.

5. T & S → i) oral skills [nec for speclst]
      ii) clarify own ideas
      iii) balance Lctrs + reading.

Writing practice

Write a letter, advising a friend or colleague of yours about how he can best organise a tutorial group. Mention the advantage of learning in small groups.

D Practice section

1 Which of the following do you regard as the true objectives of the seminar? Put them in order according to their importance. Discuss.

  a Development of the oral discussion skills
  b Team work in solving problems
  c Encouragement of critical thinking and learning
  d Clarification of ground covered in lectures, reading and laboratory
  e Opportunity to stimulate students
  f Possibility of changing attitudes
  g Chance to release tensions (ie 'let off steam')
  h Putting things in perspective
  i Contact between student and tutor
  j Practice in preparing a paper for discussion

2 Make notes about the next tutorial or seminar you attend. Write down:

  a the objectives of the seminar
  b the activities promoted during the seminar
  c the role of tutor (including his control of the discussion), and
  d the amount of preparation necessary before the seminar.

Place a series of ticks (✓) at the side of the name of each person who speaks, according to the number of statements or contributions which they make. Finally, assess the value of the tutorial/seminar.

3 Skim through the following extract from *What's the Use of Lectures?* by Donald Bligh (Penguin) in order to find three benefits of the small, informal discussion groups referred to as 'buzz groups'. Use the search-reading techniques described in Unit 7. The maximum time allowed is 60 seconds.

    'Just as individual tutorials and counselling provide a confidential situation between a member of staff and a student, buzz groups provide a confidential situation between a small number of students. Yet, unlike the college refectory or the union bar, they are within the total teaching situation. They provide the immediate reaction of the students to the teacher and interaction with him is immanent. Consequently they possess unique properties in their group dynamics which the teacher can use. Buzz groups may be used to release tensions because everyone has the opportunity to express them. The discipline of listening to lectures prevents the release of these tensions, the energy needs to be constructively channelled; consequently the use of buzz groups is a particularly valuable technique for bad lecturers! They may be used to work off examination nerves that prevent attention to any kind of class teaching, but problem-centred groups are usually even better.

'Buzz groups may also be used to give the flustered teacher breathing space. No doubt in the best of all possible worlds the teacher is never flustered; but some new teachers in Higher Education, thinking that they must lecture all the time, find that if a lecture starts badly they are unable to recover the situation. It is the sensitive lecturer who easily goes from bad to worse in this way. The use of buzz groups can give him time to think and recover his composure. Furthermore group work is precisely the kind of teaching in which his sensitivity is an asset.

'When buzz groups are used in this way the objective is an immediate one in terms of class management. It is only indirectly related to the objectives of the course, but such secondary objectives are none the less important in the long run.

'The same confidentiality and release of tension may encourage the reticent student to put his ideas into words. He is therefore more likely to be listened to, heeded and accepted by a small group. Each of these gives encouragement. With the prior agreement of his group, he is more likely to risk a contribution to the whole class at the reporting back stage or in a larger group. Since most forms of student assessment and selection place a heavy emphasis on verbal ability, and "the ability to express oneself" is an important objective of most teaching, buzz groups have an important role with the sensitive student. Since his pattern of college behaviour (which may be quite different from his behaviour at home) is probably established in his first term, buzz groups may be particularly important at that time.'

Now write down the three benefits of buzz groups, using not more than 5 or 6 words for each benefit.

Unit Nine
Writing reports and articles

A Listening comprehension: Judgement skills in writing

Listen carefully to the talk which you are about to hear. Answer each question below *when you are instructed to do so*.

Judgement skills in writing

1 Give an example of the way in which the intended reader may influence the writer of a report. (Write a sentence.)

2 Complete the following sentence by writing one word to replace each blank:
   The speaker uses   *a*   'mustn't' as an example of _____

   b   'kids' as an example of _____

   and   *c*   'To start at the beginning' as an example of _____

3 Complete the following sentence by writing one word to replace the blank:
   The speaker is talking about _____ in this section of the talk.

4 Complete the following sentence by writing one word to replace the blank:
   The amount of information you will gather will _____ the amount you require for your particular purpose.

5 Write T if the following statement is true or F if it is false:
   Provided that you have a good model, a plan is not necessary for the writing of a report.

6 The following 'model' of the talk which you have just heard is incomplete. Replace each box by the appropriate word.

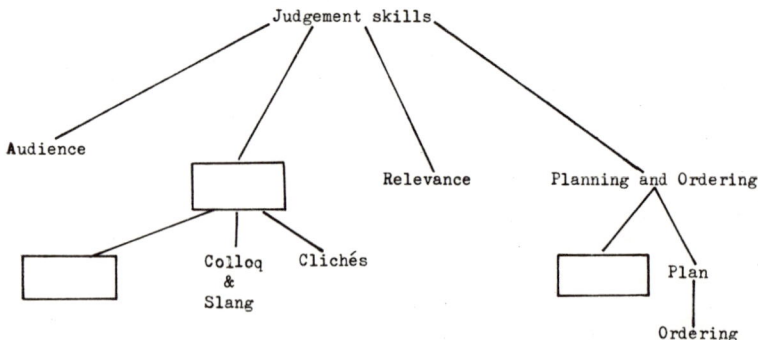

```
                        Judgement skills
              /           |          \           \
        Audience          |       Relevance    Planning and Ordering
                     [          ]                  /         \
              /       |        \             [        ]     Plan
        [      ]    Colloq    Clichés                         |
                     &                                     Ordering
                   Slang
```

B Note-taking: Relationships (3)

The following words and symbols are used to relate phrases to phrases, clauses to
  clauses, and sentences to sentences:

1 & and (also), as well as; in addition, moreover
      (Used earlier in some notes in this book.)
        Models and plans are essential in the writing of reports.
        Models & plans = essen in report writing.
        Colloquialisms as well as slang should be avoided in formal writing.
        Avoid colloqs & slang in formal writing.

2 <u>&</u> not only ... but also
        It is necessary to know precisely not only your audience but also your
        purpose in writing.
        Must know audience <u>&</u> purpose.

3 but but, yet, although; however, nevertheless; while, whereas
        Although appropriate in conversations and informal letters,
        contractions are out of place in formal writing.
        Contrctns = approp in converstns & inf letters but not in formal
        wrtng.
        Diagrams are of great use in conveying detailed statistical data in
        clear and concise terms. However, the actual description of the
        various stages of an experiment is better achieved by means of a text
        than by means of diagrams.
        Diagrams = <u>useful</u> for giving detailed stats but descr of exprmnt
        ↗ if by text.

4 or or, whether ... or
        An abstract or a summary is useful in enabling the reader to find out
        quickly and easily what the report is about.
        Abstract or summary helps reader to find contents of report.
        A sub-title can be used to expand or modify the main title.
        Sub-title can expand or modify main t.

5 <u>or</u> either ... or
        Either underlining important words and statements or taking notes
        from the text is beneficial: both methods, however, are uneconomical.
          Underlining of text <u>or</u> note-taking = useful.
        Note
        Do not confuse *or* with *or else* (meaning *unless*).
        Most students need to take notes or else they will soon forget the
        contents of the lecture.
        Must take notes or forget lecture.   (Ambiguous)
        Unless take notes, forget lecture.   (Better)

6 > is more than, is bigger than, exceeds

The objective of a tutorial should be related to acquiring skill in
discussing and thinking more than to imparting information.
Aim of tutrl – should discuss & think > give inf.
Tutorials appeared to be far more popular than lectures.
Tutrls = <u>pop</u> > lectrs.

7   <   is less than, are fewer than, is smaller than
There must be fewer students for tutorial groups than for lecture groups.
Stdnts in tutrls must be < for lectrs.
Oral discussion skills are by no means inferior to the writing skills.
Oral discsn skills ≮ writing skills.

C Reading: Report writing

Survey the following text, applying search-reading techniques in order to find out as
quickly as possible any advice which the writer gives on the ordering of material in
the main body of a report. (Make a note of the time taken to obtain the required
information.)

Report writing

The term *report* can be used to refer to a memorandum, an article for inclusion in a
specialist journal, a paper prepared for submission at a conference, a dissertation, or
a thesis. Generally, a report provides information concerning a piece of research, the
development of a project, or the result of an experiment or survey. Although it is
generally written to present information in an objective manner, the report can
sometimes be written for the primary purpose of persuading or convincing its
readers. Unlike the literary essay or topical article, however, it is rarely written for a
general audience. Indeed, it is essential that the report writer has some detailed
knowledge about his readers (usually specialists in a certain field).

   Although a report may be arranged in various ways, the basic framework for most
reports consists of:

1 the title	5 the conclusion
2 the abstract	6 the appendix
3 the introduction	7 the references
4 the main body	8 footnotes

1 *The title*. This should be as brief as possible without appearing too vague. It
should neither be ambiguous nor convey inaccurate information: for instance, it
is misleading to imply a broad coverage of a particular field when only one or two
aspects are being treated. A report on the lack of adequate parking facilities in
large cities should not be entitled simply *Traffic Problems*: a precise title would be
much more useful. If the title is long, it is better rewritten in the form of a fairly
short (general) title with a sub-title serving to expand or modify the main title.

Capital letters are generally used in titles: the first letter of nouns, verbs, adjectives and most adverbs is written in capitals, but determiners (eg *a, the, some, this*), prepositions and auxiliaries generally begin with small letters in a title.

2 *The abstract.* The abstract or summary is probably the most widely read part of the report. An abstract summarises the contents of the report by indicating the ground which is to be covered and the conclusions which will be reached. An abstract may sometimes be little more than a Table of Contents. For example, the following abstract for this reading text does not convey much more information than that conveyed by a Table of Contents:

> The article discusses report writing with an emphasis on the technical report. Details are given concerning the writing of a suitable title, the abstract, the introduction, the main body of the report, the conclusion, the appendix, references and footnotes. The article concludes with advice on the drafting of reports and proof reading.

The preceding abstract gives the reader very little information concerning the text of the report and is by no means as informative as the following version:

> The article discusses report writing with an emphasis on the technical report. After stressing the importance of brief but accurate titles, the writer concludes that the abstract is widely read because it summarises the information presented in the report. The introduction differs from typical essay introductions in so far as it usually states briefly what the report is about and the reason for writing the report. The body of the report is then treated, various methods of ordering the material being given. The reader is advised to number each point clearly and to use appropriate headings. The conclusion shows the results of the work done and often makes recommendations. Acknowledgements are included either at the end of the conclusion or separately before the appendices and reference sources. The article finishes with advice on the drafting of reports and the subsequent proof reading involved.

Although the abstract appears at the beginning of the report, it should not be written until completion of the final version. However, too many report writers use abstracts as excuses to add afterthoughts (in the same way in which postscripts in letters are added). The abstract should contain only the information in the report, presenting each point in the same order in which it will appear in the main body of the report. Abstracts are rarely written in note-form; nevertheless, they should be reasonably brief, averaging not more than 10% of the space devoted to the complete report.

3 *The introduction.* The introduction to a report is usually fundamentally different from the type of introduction generally recommended in essay writing. When learning to write an essay, students are often advised to start with a relevant proverb, quotation, anecdote, or dialogue. However, the beginning of a report should consist of a brief introduction to the subject and a statement concerning

its treatment in the report. Proposals and hypotheses should be clearly stated. The introduction provides an opportunity to state briefly the report writer's reason for writing the report. Above all, the object of the report should be stated in language and terminology based on assumptions of the reader's background knowledge.

4 *The main body*. The body of the report should be clearly set out in appropriate divisions and sub-divisions. Numbers are particularly useful as both Arabic and Roman numerals can be employed: eg 1(i), 1(ii), 2(i). The use of letters in combination with numbers is recommended since this allows for a fairly complex system of cross-referencing. Good spacing and the underlining of headings will add greatly to the visual structure of the report. Indentation also helps in enabling the reader to find his way quickly through the report, recognising relationships and the relative importance of the various sections.

Sketches are useful for treating sections of machinery, equipment and apparatus; diagrams, tables, charts and graphs are generally of far greater use than a long text in conveying detailed statistical data in clear and concise terms. However, the actual description of an experiment and the various stages of an investigation are much better achieved through a text than through diagrams. Although such steps are clearly best described in the order in which they occurred, the arrangement of material according to a chronological sequence is by no means the only way in which it can be ordered. Gradual progression from the general to the particular may be a useful means of describing new equipment or apparatus; in psychology or studies involving case histories, progression from the particular to the general may be more appropriate. Spatial organisation (following the order in which things are seen or experienced) is another method of arranging material, generally proving useful in the description of a building or a workshop.

5 *The conclusion*. This section should not contain any new material. The conclusion, often in the form of a summary, presents an opportunity to state clearly the results of the work covered in the main body of the report. Deductions and inferences can now be made and conclusions drawn. Sometimes recommendations are advanced at this stage, although certain report writers use a separate section for their recommendations. Whether appearing in the conclusion itself or immediately following it, all recommendations should be carefully worded. In many reports a separate (short) paragraph, numbered for quick reference, is devoted to each recommendation made. Unless a separate section before the appendices and reference sources is devoted to acknowledgements, the final part of the summary is an appropriate place to acknowledge briefly any assistance obtained.

6 *The appendix*. One method of presenting detailed information or statistical data is by means of an appendix. An appendix, though rarely of vital importance to the report, presents details of a particular aspect of the report without distracting the reader from the development of the argument of the report. In this way the reader

is not compelled to read the appendix unless he wants the particular information contained in it. If there are several appendices in the report, it is advisable to head each one clearly; eg Appendix A, Appendix B.

7 *References.* References to sources of information are best included in a separate section at the end of the report. They are useful not only as a means of acknowledging assistance from other reports and books but also as a means of informing the reader of useful works which he will be able to consult. When a reference is made to a report or a book, give the title, the edition and year, the author's surname and initials, the publisher (unless a report or journal) and a reference to the appropriate pages. Accuracy is essential in showing references.

8 *Footnotes.* Sometimes it is necessary to use footnotes in reports. A footnote is used to refer to other reports and findings or to elaborate on one of the points made. An asterisk (*) or a number in the body of the text (^{1}) is used to indicate a footnote at the bottom of the page. Although footnotes should be included at the foot of each page on which they occur, it is sometimes advisable to read a footnote at the end of a section or chapter so that the continuity of the report is not interrupted.

A report differs from a school essay in that it is generally the product of several draft versions. Few writers sit down and produce a report without any amendments and revision. Most report writers, in fact, produce at least two or three draft versions, writing their first draft as quickly as possible and recording whatever enters their head, provided that it is in accordance with their model or plan. Having completed this stage, however, they proceed to examine this draft very carefully indeed. In rewriting the report, they now omit and add entire sections, reshaping the material until they are satisfied with the way in which it is presented. During the next rewriting, they are thus able to concentrate chiefly on the language and style used.

One final point: the report is not completed when it is sent to the typist. It is only completed after it has been returned from the typist and read very slowly and carefully for errors and omissions. The report should be read word by word, and an attempt made to ignore the actual meaning of each statement. Proof reading is not the most interesting stage of report writing, but it is a necessary one. It is just as much the report writer's responsibility as any of the earlier stages.

Note-taking practice
Now reread the complete text carefully and make notes.

NOTES

Report Writing
Introduction
    'Report' = memo, article, thesis, etc.
            Gives inform re research, exp, survey.
            Rpt writer must know audience.

1. Title

Brief but <u>not</u> vague, ambig, inaccurate.
Long title → ↗ if short title + sub-title.
Capitals [but not for detmnrs, preps, auxils].

2. Abstract

Summary of report — should convey inform
                [not be just Table of Cntnts].
Written last but appears first.
Not like PS in letters.

3. Introduction

≠ intro to essay.
Should state propsls, hypotheses & give <u>reason</u> for report.

4. Main body

i) Divsns & sub-dvsns:
  Use of numbers: 1 i), 1 ii), 2 i) & Letters.
  Indentations ↗ recogn of relationships & imp points.
ii) Illustrations:
  a) Sketches — machinery.
  b) Diagrams, tables — stat data.
     BUT words = > for descr of exp or survey stages.
iii) Ordering:
  a) Chron order.
  b) Gen → partic [descr of equipment] <u>or</u>
            partic → gen [case histories]
  c) Spatial orgnstn [descr of workshop, etc.]

5. Conclusion

Opportnty to give results of work — deductions, infernces.
Recommendtns made here or in sep section.
Acknowldgmnts of help etc. at end of c.

6. Appendix

Can give details & stats in appndx.
A. not distract fr cont of report.
Label clearly : Appndx A, B, etc.

7. References

Best in sep sctn at end of rprt.
Acknowledge books, reports — inform reader of
sources he can consult.
i) Title   ii) edition   iii) author's name
iv) publ   v) page nos
accuracy = essential.

8. Footnotes

> To refer to other reports, etc. or to elab point made.
> Asterisk or no.
> Always put at bottom of page, but sometimes
> wait until end of section to read.

Conclusion

> Report = several drafts
> 1) Quick rough draft.
> 2) Examine & rewrite – omit/add sections.
> 3) Concen now on lang.
> Proof rdng = unint but <u>nec</u>.

Writing practice

Use the notes to write a brief report setting out guide-lines for good report writing.
(Describe briefly the audience for whom the report is intended.)

D Practice section

1 The first of the following sets of 'notes' has been assembled on a card from outline
notes taken during a lecture and later discussion in a tutorial. The second set has
been collected over a short period, based on notes made from one or two books.
Both sets of notes concern teaching in higher education. Read through them
carefully before attempting to compile three plans based on the points you would
include if you were:

  i   advising a new lecturer concerning the organisation and conducting of
      tutorials;
  ii arguing on the value of the lecture as a teaching instrument in higher
      education; and
  iii summarising the main points in both sets of notes in a single paragraph for
      future reference.

  a Is the lecture the most suitable method? – organisation of lectures and clear
     presentation are important – place for diagrams, handouts, etc – importance
     of allowing time for questions – purposes for which lectures are most suited
     (stimulate, inform, etc) – tutorial useful if tutor not dominate too much –
     should lead discussion but not assume voice of authority – preparation
     necessary on part of students – papers are one means of ensuring that certain
     amount of written work is done – group discussion can be stimulating – place
     of note-taking in tutorials and seminars not yet examined – tutor must ensure
     tutorial is relevant to needs and interests of students – practice in oral
     discussion is very useful – tutorial can also encourage intelligent reading in
     preparation for discussion.

b   Tutorials and seminars replacing many lectures – student participation – can tutorials be combined with lectures? – value of working in groups – stimulated by other students – tutorial encourages student to think – especially useful if following a 'difficult' lecture – at least one student should prepare material before tutorial – useful if asked to be group leader – but must draw out shy members of group – all members can soon work at group speed (different from individual speeds?) – tutorials best held in small rooms with seats in circle or semi-circle – seating in lecture is also important – foreign learners near front – lecturer not separated from class – importance of clear presentation and careful ordering of points in lecture.

2   Contractions, colloquialisms, slang, archaisms, clichés, proverbs, and idioms should occur neither in reports nor in formal letters. Rewrite the following letter in good English:

Dear Sir,

Books on Study Skills

I'd like to order a copy of the following books on study skills:
"Language and Study" by E V Nashbit (Littleboy)
"Advanced Skills in Study" by H A Watt (Green)

I'm enclosing a postal order for £1.40 to cover the cost of these books and estimated postage. I trust that this order will be O.K. and that you'll forward the books to me ere the end of this month.

Please note that I'm interested in any other suitable book on study skills but am completely at sea as far as knowing which are the cream of the books. As my colleagues are at sixes and sevens concerning this subject, I'd be more than grateful for any advice.

If you don't have any in stock right now, could you please pass the word to me whither I can come across such books?

Yours sincerely,

Tom P Smithson

---

3 *a*   The following model was drawn up as the basis for a brief article on *Formal Letter Writing*. Use it to write a plan on the topic.

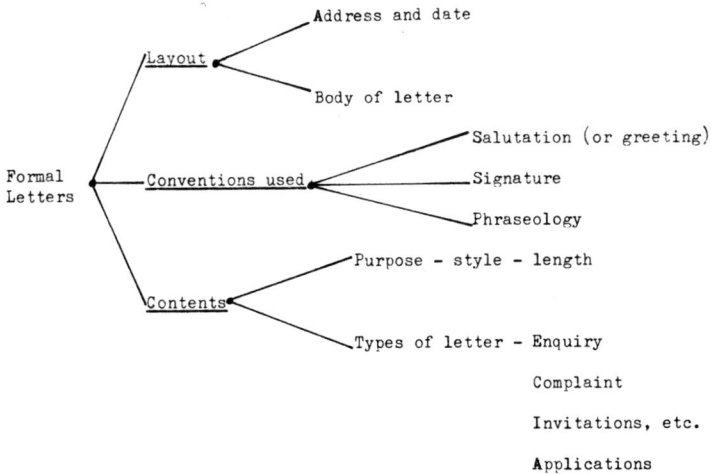

```
                                    Address and date
                      Layout
                                    Body of letter

                                          Salutation (or greeting)
Formal        Conventions used           Signature
Letters                                   Phraseology

                                    Purpose - style - length
              Contents
                                    Types of letter - Enquiry

                                                      Complaint

                                                      Invitations, etc.

                                                      Applications
```

b   The following 'notes' have been made to provide the basis for a plan of an article on the *Informal Memo*. Put them in some kind of logical order and write the plan.

When the informal memo is used – audience (ie types of readers) – typical subjects contained in memos – what constitutes a memo – classifying and filing information in memos – collection of material, facts, etc – style of memo – structure of memo (shape and length) – selection of material.

Unit Ten
Learning and remembering

A Listening comprehension: Memory

Listen carefully to the talk which you are about to hear. Answer each question below *when you are instructed to do so*.

Memory

1 According to what you have just heard, write T if the following statement is true or F if it is false:

Memory should be regarded primarily as a mental faculty.

2 Complete the following sentence by writing one word to replace the blank:

Memory is an _____.

3 Complete the table below as an example:

Witnessing an accident

Phase of memory	*Activity*
First	_____
Second	_____
Third	Remembering

4 Complete this sentence by writing several words.

The more active the learning process, _____

5 Mention some of the factors which influence the remembering phase.

6 Choose the best answer, *a, b* or *c*:

The important factor in the early stages of learning is

   a our previous experience.

   b our knowledge of note-taking techniques.

   c our ability to select.

7 Complete the following 'model' according to what you have just heard:

Remembering $\left\{ \begin{array}{l} \underline{\hspace{3cm}} \\ \underline{\hspace{3cm}} \end{array} \right.$

B Note-taking: Relationships (4)

1   ɔ   if, on condition that, provided that, so long as, supposing

> If a person has a good auditory memory, he will be able to remember things which he hears.
> ɔ auditory memory, can remember what is heard.
> We can remember material much better if we learn by wholes.
> Can remember ↗ ɔ learn by wholes.

2   <u>ɔ</u>   even if

> There is selection taking place even if a person takes down in shorthand most of what is spoken in a lecture.
> Selctn <u>ɔ</u> we note in shorthand most of lecture.
> Overlearning consists of continuing to recall the material being learnt even if we can recall it 100% correctly.
> Overlearning = recalling material <u>ɔ</u> can recall 100% correctly.

3   ∮   unless, if not

> Overlearning is useful unless it is carried to extremes.
> Overlearning = useful ∮ extremes.
> Mnemonics are fairly useful if it is not possible to use meaningful associations.
> Mnemonics = <u>useful</u> ∮ meaningful assocs.
> Students will benefit very little from lectures unless they can take good notes.
> Students not benefit fr lectures ∮ take good notes.

4   ~   varying, changing, fluctuating, differing;

varied, diverse, various, changeable;
variation, variety, change

> There are various ways in which students can prepare for the examination: syllabuses, book lists, and past examination papers all help to show the ground covered in a course.
> = ~ methods of prep for exam: syllabuses,
>   book lists,
>   exam papers.

5   ⤳   varies with, changes according to

> Reading techniques change according to the type of material being read.
> Reading techniques ⤳ texts read.

C Lecture: Methods of improving learning procedures

NOTES

Methods of Improving Learning Procedures

Intro
   Memory ↗ courses but not poss ↗ gen m.
   But can ↗ learning procedures.

1. Survey material & organise.
   Questions re material : how much nec remember?
   Select w purpose in mind.
   ∴ Arrange mat systmtclly.

2. Learn by wholes.
   Must work from gen plan [C.A. Mace — Learn by wholes]
   ∅ learn by wholes lose perspective.
   Parts of subj need atten >others but whole method=best
   [eg note-taking —signs].

3. Use of assocs.
   i) Mnemonics : e.g. cranial nerves

   ii) Meaningful assocs = △ = ↗ retention ∴ one idea → another

4. Learning by heart.
   Selected & Ltd. [Must learn formulae, dates, etc.].
   Learn in ↓ periods.
   Over learning ↗ retention.

5. Intention to learn.
   Learn ↗ ⊃ intend to learn.
   Forget ∴ want to [Freud]
   ∴ remember ∴ want to
                & intend to.

Writing practice

Use the notes to write an informal letter to a friend of yours who is interested in ways of improving his memory. Dissuade him from taking a memory improvement course and point out some of the weaknesses of 'artificial' remembering devices.

D Practice section

Examine the following sets of information. Look at each set for the time stated in brackets and attempt to remember it.

1   Departure times of buses:

   a   0623   0723   0823   0843   0923   1023

        0653   0753   0833   0853   0953   1057

        (30 secs)

   b   0613   0726   0839   0900   0952   1026

        0652   0739   0852   0926   1013   1052

        (30 secs)

2 *a*   Lieg ist parle rupo centrim aus zita tesh gelerd

       (30 secs)

  b   Since motives and feelings are involved in learning, it is only to be expected that a student will be more successful in a subject in which he is interested than in one which he finds uninteresting.

       (30 secs)

3 *a*   Memory is not a mental faculty – Learning is the first phase of memory – Selection of the material to be learnt is very important – Remembering can take the form of recognition and recall – Learning is essentially an activity – Different kinds of memory (visual, auditory, kinaesthetic, etc) – Little is known about retention because it is not observable – Deduction and inference assist recall – Learning increases if there is a sense of purpose – Remembering is the third phase of memory but changes in recall do occur.

       (60 secs)

  b   Memory $\neq$ mental faculty

       Diff kinds of 'memory' (visual, aud, kinaesthetic)

       Learning = essen activity

        i   Learning = 1st phase of memory

       ii   Retaining: little known ∵ not observable

      iii   Remembering = 3rd phase but changes in recall occur

                       = recogntn & recall

                        Recall ↗ by deductn & inference

                        Selectn of mat = <u>imp</u>

       (60 secs)   Learning ↗ ɔ sense of purpose

Write brief comments on the preceding exercises, showing their usefulness/lack of usefulness in the light of what you have learned about remembering.

Unit Eleven
Examinations

A Listening comprehension: Preparing for the examination

Listen carefully to the talk which you are about to hear. Answer each question below *when you are instructed to do so*.

Preparing for the examination

1 It is possible to prepare for an examination at the beginning of a course by adopting some of the methods outlined below. Write down each method which the speaker has mentioned.
- *a* Study book lists
- *b* Meet old students
- *c* Obtain past examination papers
- *d* Check the present syllabus
- *e* Discuss the syllabus with lecturers
- *f* Practise examination techniques

2 Choose the best answer, *a, b* or *c*:
  If you write outline notes for each question, you will
- *a* have no true indication at all of what you can do.
- *b* be able to find out weak areas in your knowledge.
- *c* not derive as much benefit as you would by writing out each answer in full.

3 Complete the following sentence by writing one word to replace each blank:
  Students should _____ their _____ evenly throughout the course.

4 What does active revision often require? Write a sentence according to what you have just heard.

5 Complete the following sentence:
  The different interests of the participants in a group will provide _____

B Note-taking: Lectures and books

When taking notes in a lecture, listen very carefully and *think* about what is being said. In this way, you can attempt to identify each important point and its relationship with other points, distinguishing it from the mass of illustrative and supporting detail surrounding it. As soon as you can – simultaneously if possible – make a brief note of the point. If, however, a part of the lecture contains a high degree of factual information (eg statistical data, formulae, dates, definitions), write *all* the facts down immediately without necessarily reflecting on their full significance. Even if the lecturer neglects to explain these facts, you can always study them carefully and check them after the lecture. Whatever information you select for your notes, concentrate primarily on writing headings, underneath which you can include brief explanations or one-word examples. Make a note, too, of any useful terminology and references to source material included in the lecture.

Remember that notes from reading are best taken after the whole of the relevant section of a textbook has been read. (The section for study may be a paragraph or a chapter and may vary in length from half a page to twenty or thirty pages.) Do *not* take notes while you are reading the section for the first time. If you adopt the SQ3R method of approaching a textbook, you will be far better able to identify the important points and see them in perspective *before* taking notes. You will also be able to turn back where necessary to check and confirm your impression of the contents of the section.

C Reading: Examination and test techniques

Skim through the following text on examination and test techniques, applying search reading strategies to obtain information about the question of *timing in both subjective examinations and objective tests.* After making a note of the time taken to obtain the required information, write a brief paragraph commenting on the importance of the time element, comparing the advice given to students with regard to the time factor in examinations and in tests.

Examination and test techniques
Introduction
Although there are several different types of examinations, each type can be classed under one of two broad headings: subjective and objective. Many students and teachers distinguish between these two categories by reserving the term 'examination' to denote assessment involving subjective judgement and the term 'test' to denote assessment by completely objective methods. Since all examinations and tests require candidates to exercise a subjective judgement and since a sampling of the contents always necessitates a subjective approach on the part of the examiner, the terms 'subjective' and 'objective' refer solely to the scoring of the answers. The actual point at which a test becomes objective is not always easy to define: on the whole, however, a test is described as being objective if it has only one correct answer. Although much the same approach is required in answering both types of papers, there are a few

major differences. Thus, it is considered advisable to treat the two separately as far as answering techniques are concerned.

Examinations

A first glance at the question paper in a subjective-type examination is often a traumatic experience for any student. The questions seem either too difficult or else different from the topics revised. A natural reaction is to search desperately for one question that can be answered instead of reading carefully through the whole paper from the first question to the last. Before glancing at the paper as a whole and considering the topics covered by the questions, the student should first read the instructions or rubrics very carefully indeed, making a note of what choice is available to him. Indeed, it is quite possible that some questions may at first appear to concentrate on a topic other than that which they actually concern.

It is now important to select and mark with a tick those questions which can best be answered. Before immediately choosing the easiest question, the student would do well to remember that higher standards will probably be required as a result of its simplicity. On the other hand, it is also inadvisable to select the most difficult question in the hope that the examiner will award marks for bravery! Most students find it good for their morale to answer first that question which they feel they can answer the best: it is always good to start any task by doing something well.

Each question should be read very carefully before an answer is even planned. The student should make sure that he understands the precise meaning of the instructions. The significant words in the question should be considered: eg

a   Describe, Show, Explain, Account for, Give an account of, Survey, Trace, Define;

b   Compare, Contrast, Discuss, Argue;

c   Enumerate, Analyse, List, Prove;

d   Assess, Evaluate, Comment (on), Criticise.

There is a tendency among many students to reproduce in an examination information which they have previously prepared for a certain topic. The student should, therefore, check very carefully before he regurgitates those answers which he has already written at some earlier stage in the course. It is highly likely that the question will differ subtly from the one for which the answer was originally prepared.

It is not advisable to write at great length on a particular subject simply for the sake of quantity: rarely do quantity and quality go hand in hand. If the student writes too much on one or two questions, he is generally left without enough time for the remaining questions. One question which has been fully answered will not obtain as high a score as two questions which have been half answered. However sympathetic an examiner might be, it is impossible for him to award marks for a question which has not been answered, even if the student has so obviously run out of time. Consequently, timing is extremely important in an examination. If the student is short of time, he should attempt to jot down the main ideas of his answer in outline form. No student, however, should become too worried if he is a little behind time in the first part of the examination: it takes a while to warm up. Nevertheless, he should take note of the time periodically and attempt to work at a steady pace within the period allotted for each question. Five minutes should then be set aside at the end of the examination for checking the answers and for finding spelling errors and any points which have been omitted.

It is advisable to draft brief outline plans of each answer before actually beginning to write out the answer to the first question. Such an approach enables the student to avoid duplicating information and to get the 'feel' of the paper and thus 'warm up'. Too often, lengthy, irrelevant introductions are a sign that a student has lacked a warming up period. Furthermore, outline plans or notes help the student to organise his material and to select the relevant from the less relevant.

Neat and legible handwriting is very important. Although the question of handwriting is a constant source of embarrassment to examiners, it has been shown that identical answers sometimes result in different marks when one answer is written neatly and clearly while the other is in poor, untidy handwriting. Good handwriting invariably influences examiners, especially in essay-type examinations, in which subjective judgements play such an important part. Spelling and punctuation are also important in determining the mark awarded.

On finishing the examination paper, the student should carefully check his answers: a careless error or a misinterpretation may appear at this stage. Finally, all the answers should be numbered correctly and the candidate's name, along with relevant details, should be written clearly at the top of his answer sheets.

The following questions on study skills are given as an example of a subjective-type examination:

Answer Questions 1 or 2 and any THREE others. (Time allowed: 2 hours)

1. Outline the various factors involved in the attainment of study objectives, commenting on the relative importance of each factor.
2. 'The ideal time to study is late at night.' Comment on this statement.
3. Analyse some of the more common types of signalling devices which operate in lectures, indicating how these can be mastered by the foreign learner.
4. Describe fully a useful approach to the learning of vocabulary for reading improvement purposes.
5. Compare a reading course which places emphasis on speed with one which stresses the importance of attaining a flexible approach to reading.
6. Enumerate the uses of a good dictionary, attempting to evaluate each use.
7. What can the lecture achieve?
8. Account for the widespread popularity of the SQ3R method, showing its importance in higher education.
9. List the major benefits of the tutorial system.
10. Compare the techniques required for the writing of technical reports with those required for the writing of essays.

Tests

Most objective questions test recognition: the multiple-choice type requires the candidate to recognise the correct answer from a choice of 4 or 5 possible answers. Some objective tests, however, are used to test recall: completion items require the candidate to complete an incomplete statement by supplying the correct answer.

Because the questions contained in the paper can usually be answered very rapidly, most objective tests cover a wide area of knowledge. In this way, an objective test can make far greater demands on a student than an essay-type examination, even though it may appear rather easy at first sight. The fact that a wide sample of the student's knowledge is covered in a short time is one reason for the popularity of objective tests among teachers, even though there is virtually no emphasis on the manipulation of language and ideas in objective tests.

While certain objective tests penalise students for guessing by deducting marks for wrong answers, a few others appear to encourage 'cautious' guessing. Consequently, it is of vital importance for the student to check the instructions at the outset in order to determine whether guessing is penalised. If the instructions omit any reference to guessing, the student should be prepared to guess on occasions, provided that he does not guess blindly and bases his guesses on partial knowledge. Guesses based on what a student knows or what he can deduce are an important part of the learning process. Few students are foolish enough to indulge in guesswork without any basis of reason or deduction.

Very few objective tests allow for choice, but again the instructions should be carefully checked to clarify this point. Different types of questions appearing on the same paper will necessitate changes in the instructions. It is thus advisable to glance through not only the instructions in the paper, but also the total number of questions. It is unnecessary, however, to read through the paper in the same way in which the subjective paper is read. A quick glance will generally be enough to acquaint most candidates with the types of questions and different instructions.

The ability to read with care and comprehension is often very important in objective tests: an awareness of the use of such modifiers as *sometimes, usually, rarely, always* and *never*, for example, can make all the difference between selecting a correct answer and an incorrect one.

After having surveyed the paper and read the instructions very carefully, the student should proceed to work through the test systematically, periodically checking the time. If he finds himself working on one question for much longer than the allotted time, he should leave it and proceed to the next question, being prepared to return later to the question he finds more difficult.

Although it is misleading to regard objective tests as synonymous with multiple-choice tests, the multiple-choice item is an effective way of testing knowledge of a particular subject. Note that the word *item* is preferred to *question* since a multiple-choice test may take the form of either *a* a question followed by 4 or 5 possible answers (= options) or *b* an incomplete statement with

4 or 5 possible ways of completing it: eg

   a Why is note-taking very useful in the learning process?

    A It helps the student to participate actively in learning.

    B It provides the student with excellent practice in writing.

    C It improves the student's understanding of what the lecturer is saying.

    D It develops the student's creative powers.

   b In order to gain interest in an uninteresting subject we should try to

    A increase our span of attention in the subject.

    B remember the most important information in the subject.

    C take useful notes on the subject.

    D relate the subject to something we find interesting.

Note that it is usually not difficult in multiple-choice items to transform questions into incomplete statements: eg

   a What should the student do as soon as possible after a lecture?

    A He should relax for a short while.

    B He should prepare for the next lecture.

    C He should read through the notes he has taken.

    D He should try to attend a tutorial.

   b As soon as possible after a lecture the student should

    A relax for a short while.

    B prepare for the next lecture.

    C read through the notes he has taken.

    D try to attend a tutorial.

    Other objective-type items are:

1 the true/false item:

    Write T if each of the following statements is true and F if it is false:

   a A good dictionary prescribes rules about which words we use.

   b Most dictionaries do not include regional variations of language.

   c Dictionaries soon become out of date because the language of a community is always changing.

2 the completion item:

    Complete the following sentence by writing one word in each blank:

    Important points in a lecture can be easily identified if the student is _____ with the subject of the lecture and he is aware of the various s_____ d_____.

3 the matching item:

    Arrange each phrase in *List B* with the correct word in *List A*.

List A	List B
1 Survey	Most active stage
2 Question	Skim chapters
3 Read	Repetition of first four steps
4 Recall	Adopt a critical attitude
5 Revise	Answer questions now

4   Rearrangement:
     The following steps should be carried out in an examination. Put them in their
     correct order:
          Check answers for omissions and errors.
          Write outline plans for the questions.
          Read and answer the first question.
          Select the questions to be answered.
          Check the time periodically.
          Read all the questions.

Conclusion

Most subjective examinations allow for a choice of topics while very few objective
tests allow for any choice whatsoever. Moreover, such features as legible and neat
handwriting are generally less important in objective tests since the correct answer is
usually denoted by the insertion of a word or by a tick. Reading comprehension is
possibly a more important skill than writing in an objective test. However, the
subjective examination places far greater emphasis on the communication of ideas.
The importance of timing is common to both, while the careful reading of
instructions and the initial survey of the paper are also essential in both subjective
examinations and objective tests.

Note-taking practice

Now reread the complete text carefully and make notes.

NOTES

<u>Examination and Test Techniques</u>

<u>Intro</u>
     Subj [=exams] and obj [=tests].
     But stdnt must ex subj judgmnt in both
          also sampling of contents = subj.
          Only marking = obj ∴ only 1 correct answ.

<u>Exams</u>
     1. Many search desprtly + not survey whole paper.
        Must 1st read instrctns + note choice, etc.
     2. i) Select questions + mark.
          [Beware ⚠ easy + ⚠ difficult.]

ii) Ans best question 1st.
iii) ↑ words in question : e.g. describe, compare, analyse, assess.
iv) Not reproduce 'set' topic.
3. i) Quality > qntty.
   ⊃ ↑ time on 1 qstn ⟶ ↓ time on others.
   ii) Timing = imp [∴ 2 qstns ½ answd > 1 full a].
   ⊃ ↓ time, jot down main ideas.
   Note time periodclly.
   Keep 5 mins for checking at end.
4. Brief plans = underline{useful}
              ∴ i) warm up
                 ii) organise material and select relevant inf.
5. Good handwrtng = imp [also spelling + punctuation].

Tests

1. Most test recogn [M/c tests]
   but some test recall [Compltn].
2. Cover wide area.
3. Guessing : some penalise; others encourage.
   Base guesses on part knowl + deduction.
4. Survey qstns + check instrctns.
   [Most tests - no choice]
5. Reading = imp.
   [Aware of modifiers: sometimes, etc.]
6. Work thru test systmtclly.
7. i) M/c items
   ii) T/f   "
   iii) Compltn "
   iv) Matching "
   v) Rearngmnt

Conclusion

1. Differ
   i) Obj - no choice
   ii) Obj - hndwrtng - ↘ imp
   iii) Obj - reading comprhnsn
      Subj - commun of ideas
2. Same
   i) Timing
   ii) Reading of instrctns
   iii) Survey

Writing practice

Using the notes given, write a letter to a friend, giving him advice on how to take an examination. Your friend, who is preparing for his university entrance examination at the end of the year, is rather carefree and works in fits and starts. He is really an intelligent student but he tends to rebel against authority and he resents advice when given patronisingly.

D Practice section

Complete each of the following statements by choosing the correct answer, A, B, C or D, according to what you have read in this book. (Each statement refers to information contained in the units in this book.)

Example: Students should start to prepare for an examination

    A a month before the examination.
    B at the beginning of the course.
    C half-way through the course.
    D a few days before the examination.

'B' is the correct answer.

1 Guiding the student in his work and making him aware of his progress can best be accomplished by means of

    A annual examinations.
    B continuous assessment.
    C frequent lectures.
    D interviews.

2 An interest in the subject and a desire to pass an examination can be of great use in

    A making a student aware of his progress.
    B providing motivation.
    C determining objectives.
    D overcoming feelings of strain and tension.

3 The best time to study is generally

    A in the morning.
    B in the afternoon.
    C in the early evening.
    D late at night.   .

4 Study periods should be planned so that they immediately precede

    A a lecture.
    B a seminar.
    C laboratory work.
    D an examination.

5 If the student comes across something completely unfamiliar in a lecture, he is advised to

A copy it down and check later.

B ignore it and not allow it to distract him.

C translate it into his own language.

D check it immediately by referring to a book.

6 It is not possible to isolate satisfactorily for learning purposes most of the

    A signs expressing relationships in speech and writing.

    B methods of setting out lecture notes.

    C signalling devices in lectures.

    D features of the spoken language involving word omission and compression.

7 The brief periods in which the eye stops when reading are known as

    A fixations.

    B recognition spans.

    C jerky movements.

    D word pyramids.

8 The pronouns 'the former' and 'the latter' are examples of

    A connectives.

    B expansion devices.

    C non-grammatical parts of speech.

    D reference features.

9 The primary purpose of the lecture should be

    A to convey original information and ideas.

    B to provide opportunities for group learning.

    C to stimulate and encourage students to think.

    D to enable research workers to talk about their research.

10 During a lecture it is important to

    A sit passively.

    B argue with the lecturer.

    C adopt a critical attitude.

    D keep to one's own views.

11 Lectures are far more suited than books to

    A useful note-taking.

    B providing relevant information on a subject.

    C imparting facts.

    D conveying new and difficult concepts.

12 Students dislike many lectures primarily because of

    A the poor lecturing techniques used.

    B the uninteresting subjects they concern.

    C the amount of information conveyed.

    D the personality of the teacher.

13 Dictionaries soon become out of date because

    A they have been cheaply produced.

    B they have not taken into account regional variations of language.

    C   language is constantly changing.

    D   most users fail to abide by the rules prescribed for using words.

14 Diacritical marks are used in some dictionaries to show

    A   syllable division.

    B   pronunciation.

    C   difficulties in spelling.

    D   colloquialisms.

15 Dictionaries written specially for the foreign learner are of the greatest use because

    A   they contain derivations of words.

    B   they include words needed for study at advanced levels.

    C   they use a controlled vocabulary

    D   they are compiled by native speakers of English.

16 When a person skims, his eyes often appear to move

    A   erratically down a page.

    B   horizontally in regular jumps.

    C   carefully over six lines of print.

    D   quickly but smoothly across a line.

17 In order to find if certain books contain useful information for our purposes, we need an ability to

    A   take notes.

    B   skim.

    C   remember details.

    D   adopt short-term goals.

18 Skimming techniques should be used in dealing with a textbook in the

    A   survey stage.

    B   question stage.

    C   reading stage.

    D   recall stage.

19 The most active stage of the SQ3R method is generally considered to be

    A   survey.

    B   revise.

    C   question.

    D   recall.

20 A sense of direction and purpose in reading a book usually results from

    A   glancing at the bibliography.

    B   formulating questions.

    C   taking notes.

    D   comparing it with another book.

21 After progressing through the initial stages of learning to speak a foreign language, the student should concern himself more with

    A   the correctness of his pronunciation.

B   the accuracy of the sentence structures used.

C   the comprehension of unfamiliar accents.

D   the communication of ideas.

22 In tutorials it is important that a student

    A   does not make mistakes of grammar.

    B   communicates his ideas.

    C   pronounces each word correctly.

    D   does not lose face.

23 The conclusion of the technical report is the place in which to

    A   present statistical data.

    B   advance recommendations.

    C   give sources of information.

    D   describe the various stages of an experiment.

24 The title of a report should

    A   indicate a broad coverage of the field.

    B   concentrate on a major aspect of the report.

    C   be brief but not vague.

    D   attract attention through ambiguity, etc.

25 The contents of a report are often summarised in the form of

    A   an abstract.

    B   an introduction.

    C   footnotes.

    D   an appendix.

26 Although footnotes appear at the bottom of the page in a report, many are best
read

    A   immediately.

    B   at the end of the section.

    C   after the complete report has been read.

    D   a few days afterwards.

27 Memory is best defined as being

    A   a mental faculty.

    B   an activity.

    C   a special talent.

    D   a learning experience.

28 Recall is greatly assisted by

    A   deduction and inference.

    B   frequent repetition.

    C   the use of mnemonics.

    D   recognition and identification.

29 Objective tests are distinguished from subjective examinations in so far as

    A   they are generally much easier.

    B   less time is usually required.

   C   there is often only one correct answer.
   D   they have a good effect on learning.
30 Outline plans for answers to each question in an examination are useful because
   A   they enable the student to get the feel of the paper.
   B   they give the examiner a good idea of the student's knowledge.
   C   they enable the examiner to mark the paper quickly.
   D   they give the student a better awareness of time.

After completing the test, find out how many items concerned each unit.
(Eg on which unit were most items set?)
Comment on the test as a reliable way of indicating whether or not a student has
mastered the skills practised in this book. Suggest other, more reliable means of
measuring these skills.

Unit Twelve

Reference and research techniques

A Listening comprehension: Reference techniques

Listen carefully to the talk which you are about to hear. Answer each question below *when you are instructed to do so*.

Reference techniques: Using a dictionary

1 What are the two ways in which most library books are classified?
2 Write T if the following statement is true or F if it is false:
   The speaker has briefly described the Dewey system of classification.
3 The following is the last statement the speaker made in the section you have just heard. Write one word to replace each blank:
   However, this system is not without obvious _____ because certain sections take little account of _____ and _____ factors. Many colleges and universities overseas _____ the system slightly in order to meet their own special requirements.
4 The following headings have actually been taken from a university library specialising in books on education. Has the Dewey system or the Library of Congress system been used for classification purposes?

372	THE CHILD AND SCHOOL
372.1	PRIMARY EDUCATION
372.101	CURRICULUM
372.2	JUNIOR SCHOOLS
372.22	ACTIVITY METHODS & PROJECTS
372.23	FROEBEL
372.24	INFANT & NURSERY SCHOOLS
372.244	GAMES & ACTIVITIES
372.31	SPECIAL APPROACHES (MONTESSORI, ETC)
372.4	READING

5 Choose the best answer, *a, b, c* or *d*:
   We would expect to find the following card in the

a Subject Index.
b Classified Catalogue.
c Author Catalogue.
d Title Catalogue.

EDUCATION:	fundamental	370.93
	further	374 - .99
	general writings	370.101
	girls	376 - .99
	guidance	371.42
	health	371.7 - .723
	higher	378 - .999
	history	370.9 -.99
	industrial	371.426

6 The following card could be found in two catalogues in a library. Write out the catalogue names:

```
154.4
MACE, Cecil Alex
     The Psychology of Study, by C.A. Mace.
     Newly revised (ed.)
     Harmondsworth;  Penguin, 3/6.  1968.
     128p.  18cm.  Pbk.  bibl.  p.123-125
```

B Note-taking: Sequence of ideas

In certain types of lectures, the speaker touches on a particular point only to move on to another point almost immediately. Later, however, he returns to the original point and amplifies it, often in the light of the information which he has just given to his audience. While perhaps a convenient and sometimes a necessary means of developing thoughts and ideas concerning a certain topic, such a method often makes outline notes appear disjointed and confused. Where the lecturer's amplification at a later stage is fairly brief, it is generally possible to refer back to the original point in the notes and to add the odd phrase or two on the same line: hence the value of pacing out one's notes. On the other hand, however, where the amplification is quite considerable, it is generally advisable to use a line or an arrow to show the connections and relationships between the appropriate sections of the notes.

To avoid being confused by such 'back-tracking' in lectures, the student should listen carefully to whatever clues he can pick up. It is often possible to tell when a speaker intends to return to a particular point. For example, in the listening comprehension exercise in Section A of this unit, the speaker refers to two systems of library classification (the Dewey decimal system and the Library of Congress system) before proceeding to discuss the Dewey system in some detail. Although he does not ignore the Library of Congress system for too long, it is nevertheless important for the listener to be aware of his *probable* intention to return to this subject. Consequently, instead of setting one's notes as follows:

1 Dewey system
2 Library of Congress system
1 Dewey system
   10 main classes of knowl.
Etc.

it might be preferable to set out the notes in the following way:

1 Dewey system   2 Library of Congress system
   10 main classes of knowl.
Etc.

The relevant information would then be written under the appropriate column.

Frequently, it will be necessary for the student to impose his own structure on the information obtained from a lecture. In the short lecture which follows in Section C, for example, the speaker begins by using numbers to denote the various stages involved in conducting research. However, after the third stage he forgets to introduce each stage by means of its appropriate number. In such a case, therefore, the student will continue to number each separate stage, trying to identify clearly the division between each stage. Occasionally, it will be necessary to *rewrite* the outline notes at the end of a lecture, reorganising the information and rearranging the various points. Such a task is in itself an important part of active learning and stands out in contrast to such passive methods as making neat copies of notes.

C Lecture: Research techniques

NOTES

<u>Research Techniques : Planning and Conducting Research</u>

<u>Intro</u>
    Research = system & thoro enquiry into imp qstns
         results of r→↗knowl & ↗apprectn of issues involved.
      R ⟨ acqstn of knowl
         → beyond books

Stages of Research

1. Many topics – list all.
   Make short list & discuss w tutor.
   Good libr = imp.
2. Define problem chosen = imp.
   Define clearly so can reach conclsn.
3. Observe & collect data.
   Read r papers on assoc fields ∴ inf
                                    idea of treatment.
   Card index or file.
4. Analyse data → form hypothesis.
   ⎡Method, size of sample ←— hypothesis.
   ⎣Avoid making predictns — then no bias.
5. Sampling.
   Accurate & rep s = imp. [Exclude other factors]
6. Conduct investgtn or do expmnt.
   Statistics – open to abuses: can measure other factors
   [chance etc.] & infl by prej.
7. Interptn of results of data.
   Support hypothesis & add to it.
8. Write report/thesis = imp.
   Draft form 1st.
   Remember audience and purpose.

Writing practice

Select a topic in which you are genuinely interested and would like to do research.
Imagine that you have a year in which to undertake the research you want to do.
Define the problem very clearly and write a brief account of the various stages you
envisage in your research.

D Practice section

Find the appropriate cards in your school, college or university library catalogue for
books on each of the following subjects. Write down the title of each book, its author,
publisher and classification number. (Note that most of the topics listed are related
to the contents of this book.)

1 Studying on a self-instruction basis	7 Memory
2 Freud	8 Phonology
3 English affixes	9 Modern methods of printing
4 Mental health	10 Statistical procedures in research
5 William James	11 Sleep
6 The role of motivation in learning	12 Library organisation

Bibliography

Study (General)

Beveridge, W M (1965) *The Art of Study.* London. O U P.
Bjernum, Vibeke (1971) *Study Technique – Hints for Students.* London. Harrap.

Crow, L & A (1963) *How to Study.* New York. Collier.
Guinery, M (1967) *How to Study.* London. Allen & Unwin.
James, D E (1967) *A Student's Guide to Efficient Study.* London. Pergamon.

Laing, A (1963) *The Art of Study.* Leeds. University of Leeds.

Mace, C A (1968) *The Psychology of Study.* Harmondsworth. Penguin.

Maddox, H (1963) *How to Study* (Revised edition, 1967). London. Pan.

Morgan, C T & Deese, J (1957) *How to Study.* New York. McGraw-Hill.

Rowntree, D (1970) *Learn How to Study.* London. Macdonald.

Wright, E & Wallwork, J F (1962) *On Your Own – a guide to study method.* London. Longman.

Yorkey, Richard C (1970) *Study Skills for Students of English as a Second Language.* New York. McGraw-Hill.

Note-taking

Hill, L A (1968) *Note-taking Practice.* London. O U P.

Reading techniques

Fry, Edward (1963)	*Teaching Faster Reading*. Cambridge. CUP.
Harris, D P (1966)	*Reading Improvement Exercises for Students of English as a Second Language*. Englewood Cliffs, New Jersey. Prentice-Hall.
Latham, D W (ed) (1974)	*The Road to Effective Reading*. London. Ward Lock.
Leeuw, M & E, de (1965)	*Read Better, Read Faster*. Harmondsworth. Penguin.
Pugh, A K (1973)	*Techniques for Effective Reading*. Leeds. University of Leeds.
West, M (1941)	*Learning to Read a Foreign Language*. London. Longman.

Lectures

Bligh, Donald A (1972)	*What's the Use of Lectures?* Harmondsworth. Penguin.

Report writing

Cooper, B M (1964)	*Writing Technical Reports*. Harmondsworth. Penguin.
Ehrlich, E & Murphy, D (1964)	*The Art of Technical Writing*. New York. Bantam.
Kapp, R O (1948)	*The Presentation of Technical Information*. London. Constable.

English pronunciation

Gimson, A C (1962)	*An Introduction to the Pronunciation of English* (Second edition, 1970). London. Edward Arnold.
Jones, D (1960)	*An Outline of English Phonetics*. Cambridge. Heffer.
O'Connor, J D (1967)	*Better English Pronunciation*. Cambridge. CUP.
Pring, Julian T (1959)	*Colloquial English Pronunciation*. London. Longman.

Learning techniques

Beard, Ruth (1970)

Teaching and Learning in Higher Education. Harmondsworth. Penguin.

Borger, R & Seabourne, A E M (1970)

The Psychology of Learning. Harmondsworth. Penguin.

Hunter, I M L (1964)

Memory (Revised edition). Harmondsworth. Penguin.

Examinations

Allen, C E (1963)

Passing Examinations. London. Macmillan.

Research techniques

Nisbet, J D & Entwistle, N J (1970)

Educational Research Methods. London. U L P.

The Open University (1973)

Methods of Educational Enquiry, Blocks 1–6. Milton Keynes. Open University Press.

Dictionaries, etc.

Hornby, A S (1974)

Advanced Learner's Dictionary of Current English (Third edition). London. O U P.

Hornby, A S & Parnwell, E.C. (1952)

An English-Reader's Dictionary. London. O U P.

Flood, W E & West, M (1962)

An Elementary Scientific and Technical Dictionary (Third edition). London. Longman.

Fowler, H W & F G (ed) (1911)

The Concise Oxford Dictionary of Current English (Fifth edition, revised by E McIntosh, 1964). London. O U P.

Little, W, Fowler, H W & Coulson, J (1933)

The Shorter Oxford English Dictionary (Third edition, revised and edited by C T Onions, 1964). London. O U P.

Gove, P B et al (ed) (1961)

Webster's Third New International Dictionary. London. Bell.

West, M (1965)

An International Reader's Dictionary. London. Longman.

Uvarov, E G & Chapman, D R (1943) — *A Dictionary of Science* (Revised, for the Third edition, by A Isaacs, 1964) Harmondsworth. Penguin.

Jones, D (1917) — *Everyman's English Pronouncing Dictionary* (Thirteenth edition, edited by A C Gimson, 1967). London. Dent.

Lewis, J Windsor (1972) — *A Concise Pronouncing Dictionary of British and American English*. London. O U P.

Roget, P M (1852) — *Thesaurus of English Words and Phrases* (New edition completely revised and modernised by R A Dutch, 1962). London. Longman.

Fowler, H W (1926) — *A Dictionary of Modern English Usage*. (Second edition, revised by Sir Ernest Gowers, 1965). London. O U P.

Heaton, J B & Stocks, J P (1965) — *Overseas Students' Companion to English Studies*. London. Longman.

West, M & Kimber, P F (1957) — *Deskbook of Correct English*. London. Longman.

Wood, F T (1962) — *Current English Usage*. London. Macmillan.

Appendix: Talks and lectures (Scripts)
Unit One
Study problems and objectives

A Listening comprehension

You will hear a short talk, on which you will be asked questions. The talk will be divided into sections, after each of which there will be a pause. You will be required to answer one question during each pause. (Turn off your machine while you answer.)

Study problems

1 A large number of students entering university or college experience study problems of one kind or another. Such problems are not, of course, confined to non-native speakers of English: they're faced by native speakers and by foreign learners alike. However, what constitutes a minor difficulty to the native speaker often becomes a major one to the foreign learner because of general problems of language.
Now answer question 1 in the Listening comprehension section.

2 Some students are not aware of the existence of study problems. They confuse them with academic problems or else they think that they're simply another kind of language problem. While it's impossible to separate these problems and put them into clearly-defined categories, an awareness of the nature of the actual study problem involved is essential.
Now answer question 2 in the Listening comprehension section.

3 What, then, are the chief factors which contribute to most study problems? Clearly, one important problem encountered in studying at the more advanced levels is language: quite simply, the language you require now will probably be very different from the classroom or textbook kind of English you learnt at school. In all too many schools a literary variety of English has been added to the artificial textbook variety.
Now answer question 3 in the Listening comprehension section. Then read question 4.

4 In addition to requiring a different variety of English, you will require different language skills, too. The ability to follow lectures in English and to take notes, the ability to write reports and to make valuable contributions in seminars and tutorials, and the ability to use appropriate and effective strategies for reading books and papers – all these are new abilities which you must now strive to possess.
Now answer question 4 in the Listening comprehension section.

5 In your general approach to your academic work at college or university level, you will find yourself having to meet new demands. In most schools the teacher bears the responsibility for the learning process; very often spoon-feeding takes place. In most universities and colleges, however, few concessions of this kind are made to the individual student. You will be expected to read widely and to discuss new concepts, many of which will seem totally foreign to you. Above all, you must begin to think for yourself. And you will find yourself working in a strange environment in which standards and expectations are even higher than previously.

Now answer question 5 in the Listening comprehension section.

Unit Two

Organising your study

A Listening comprehension

You will hear a short talk, on which you will be asked questions. The talk will be divided into sections, after each of which there will be a pause. You will be required to answer one question during each pause. (Turn off your machine while you answer.)

Concentration and study habits
1 Concentration varies from one individual to another. We all differ in our ability to sit down at a certain task for long periods. A few people can study one subject for a short time and then switch without any difficulty at all to another subject. But individual differences like this are not the only factor governing concentration. We must take into account the kind of study tasks being performed. Our degree of concentration will vary according to their complexity, their size *and* the terms in which they're defined. A third factor involved in concentration is fatigue: concentration must inevitably fall after a certain period of study.
   Now answer question 1 in the Listening comprehension section.
2 As we have seen, there is a strong link between concentration and interest. An interest in a subject will usually increase our span of attention and help us to remember information much more easily. If we don't feel much interest in the subject, then we ought to think about ways of relating it to a subject that does interest us.
   Now answer question 2 in the Listening comprehension section.
3 If concentration is difficult, we'll probably experience a certain initial inertia when trying to get down to serious study. Clearly defined short-term objectives will help here, for vague objectives are a great deal harder to accomplish – and so foster feelings of initial inertia. However, if we still find it difficult to study, then we can try studying only for short periods at a time. In this way, we can approach each study session in the knowledge that we're going to finish in, say, an hour. Then there'll be a sense of urgency about our work.
   Now answer question 3 in the Listening comprehension section.
4 Advice on the ideal length of time for study sessions is difficult to give, for account must be taken of each individual and the work he is engaged on. On the whole, the more advanced the field of study, the longer the time we should spend on it. It takes a certain time to warm up, especially in studying at advanced levels.

Now answer question 4 in the Listening comprehension section.

5 However, it is dangerous to generalise. Study periods involving difficult material should be short. Study periods in which a lot of information and data are memorised should also be short. On the other hand, however, study periods involving work of a more practical nature – for example, the writing up of an experiment or the reading of background material – may often be much longer. Now answer question 5 in the Listening comprehension section.

C Lecture

Listen carefully to the brief lecture I'm going to give on planning a timetable. Take outline notes of the important points.

Planning a timetable

Many students dislike the idea of keeping to a strict timetable. They feel that study at advanced levels should acquire a breadth and freedom which cannot be circumscribed by any number of detailed timetables. Other students prefer to work in cycles: after a period of doing very little work, they'll work on a particular project for days on end.

However, for most people a timetable is a valuable aid in ensuring that work is done regularly. It shouldn't be seen as a restricting force but rather as a means of enabling the student to achieve his goals. The absence of a timetable often gives rise to problems of initial inertia and uncertainty concerning objectives and priorities. Nothing can beat regular periods of study. Imagine, for instance, the amount that can be achieved if a student works at a particular topic for, say, just one hour a day for five days a week: this totals almost two hundred hours of study by the end of the academic year. There's an ancient Chinese fable about how an old man managed to move a mountain which obstructed his way to the nearest town. Each day he and his sons spent a few hours removing the earth with their spades. Although the old man never saw the result, of course, and although many generations had to carry on the work, the mountain was eventually moved.

Both long-term and short-term goals must be taken into account when the timetable is being planned. Long-term goals, however, will require long-term plans based on a sound knowledge of the syllabus, of examination requirements, and of deadlines for handing in work. After making his long-term plans, the student will be in a position to organise his short-term goals in the form of a timetable. Such a timetable must be based at the very outset on the student's knowledge of himself and his capabilities. There's a great deal of evidence, for example, to show that most people, when planning a timetable, tend to overrate the speed at which they work. It's generally a good idea to make out the timetable after the first week or so of a new course – and to be prepared to revise it at weekly or monthly intervals.

Now how long should be spent on study? The number of hours will be determined by the student's class timetable, by his own personal capabilities and by the amount of work he feels is necessary in order to achieve his objectives. However, let's take for purposes of illustration the amount of study which the average student does: the figure usually varies between forty and fifty hours a week. If a student spends fifteen hours a week attending lectures – as some arts students do – then he should reckon on roughly thirty-five hours of study a week. If he spends twenty-five hours attending lectures and working in the laboratory – as many science students do – then he should allocate about twenty-five hours a week for study.

What times of the day are best for study purposes? Many lecturers advise working at the most difficult tasks in the morning while the mind is fresh and alert. Although there's little conclusive evidence to suggest that any one time of the day is better than any other for studying, it's generally felt on psychological grounds that the morning period is best for work involving mental effort. Certain students, however, reserve their most difficult work for the night. They point out that everything is quiet then and that there are few physical distractions. Furthermore, it's now thought that slight body fatigue may even be beneficial for adopting suitable attitudes for study – provided the student doesn't attach a false glamour to burning the midnight oil and turn up for morning lectures bleary-eyed.

Study sessions during the day will depend on the class timetable. Whenever possible, it's advisable to plan a study period immediately *after* a lecture in order to review the notes taken and carry out follow-up work. In the case of a seminar, however, it's useful to arrange a study period immediately *before* so that the necessary preparation can be made.

The value of rest periods should not be overlooked. Relaxation on Saturday afternoons or evenings and on Sundays is necessary in most study programmes. In addition, it's useful on occasions for the student to offer 'rewards' to himself for having achieved certain study goals: such rewards might take the form of an evening at the cinema or at a friend's home. Moreover, the student should take a short rest whenever he feels he's becoming stale or bored with his subject: a short break in the form of a walk or a chat with friends is advisable. Finally, he should try to obtain the necessary amount of sleep at night, for it's the intensity and quality of study rather than the length which is of most importance.

Unit Three
Note-taking

A Listening comprehension

You will hear a short talk, on which you will be asked questions. The talk will be divided into sections, after each of which there will be a pause. You will be required to answer one question during each pause. (Turn off your machine while you answer.)

General principles of note-taking

1 One famous writer – I forget who it was – once said, 'The weakest ink is superior to the strongest memory.' Note-taking is an excellent illustration of this point. Outline notes of a text or a lecture provide vital help in the recall process. Not only will they emphasise the important points and ideas to be remembered but they will also show clearly how the various thoughts and arguments have been developed.
Now answer question 1 in the Listening comprehension section.

2 Note-taking, however, is also important in another way. It provides a valuable opportunity to participate actively in the learning process. Indeed, some study experts prefer the phrase *note-making* to *note-taking*, since the former implies a more active and critical attitude to study. When taking notes, you are no longer just sitting passively listening to a lecture or reading a book. You are far more deeply involved in the learning process. In this way, note-taking greatly increases your ability to concentrate.
Now answer question 2 in the Listening comprehension section.

3 The amount of notes you take depends very much on the type of lecture you attend (or the type of book you read). Some lectures may contain very little factual information, while others may be packed with factual information and statistical data. Also, your own background knowledge of the particular subject will help to determine how many notes you take.
Now answer question 3 in the Listening comprehension section.

4 There are three approaches to dealing with lectures and books. First – and at one extreme – you can take down as much as possible of the lecture or book. But lectures (even more than books) include a great deal of repetition and redundant material. When you come to revise, detailed notes will offer little guidance as to what is important and what is not. Moreover, anyone who takes full notes leaves himself with little time to reflect on the content of the lecture and digest what he's heard. A second approach to dealing with lectures and books – and at the

other extreme – is to take no notes at all and rely entirely on memory. Unfortunately, however, ideas and impressions disappear all too quickly.

Now answer question 4 in the Listening comprehension section.

5 The third course – and the most satisfactory one – is to take outline notes. This means that you must distinguish between what is important and what is not so important – and reflect on the relationship between the various ideas expressed. There is obviously a great difference here between taking notes from a book and taking notes from a lecture. In the former you should glance quickly through the relevant section before coming back to study parts of it in greater detail and take notes: in other words, you work from the general outline to the detail. In lectures, however, it is much more difficult to select what is relevant because a general picture of the subject will only emerge gradually as the lecture progresses; thus here you work from the detail to the general outline.

Now answer question 5 in the Listening comprehension section.

6 You should try to review lecture notes as soon as possible after the lecture, while the points are still fresh in your mind. Often an example or a word may stick in your mind and bring back the whole context to you. If left until a few days later, however, the significance of such a word or phrase may be forgotten. On the whole, it is advisable *not* to copy out your notes neatly: instead, read through them critically, asking yourself questions and referring to other sources such as textbooks and journals. Amplify your notes where you think necessary and add points.

Now answer question 6 in the Listening comprehension section.

7 One final word: try to avoid taking notes in your mother tongue. Such a procedure generally involves the translation of new and often difficult concepts – and this is a special skill attained only by the most competent and experienced interpreters. A word or phrase in the mother tongue, of course, may be of great value in providing a meaningful interpretation or clarification of a certain point. Provided that it is confined to such circumstances, the mother tongue will be of help in note-taking.

Now answer question 7 in the Listening comprehension section.

Unit Four

Improving your reading

A Listening comprehension

You'll hear a short talk, on which you'll be asked questions. The talk will be divided into sections, after each of which there'll be a pause. You will be required to answer one question during each pause. (Turn off your machine while you answer.)

Increasing reading speed

1 Many native speakers have been able to increase their reading speed considerably as a result of making conscious attempts to do so. A desire to read faster, combined with regular practice, will generally result in the student reading faster and still maintaining adequate comprehension for many purposes. These two factors – rather than any reliance on particular methods and gimmicks – explain why many speed reading courses can justifiably claim great success.
Now answer question 1 in the Listening comprehension section.

2 Although there has been some doubt whether the actual skills developed on many speed reading courses can be applied to real-life situations, it has been shown that, where the wide range of reading skills required by the student has been properly identified on a course, these reading skills can be used in real-life situations. A few people argue that practice aimed at reading improvement should first take place in the mother tongue rather than in English, but not enough is yet known about the transfer of training from one language to another – though there are certain indications that some transfer does take place.
Now answer question 2 in the Listening comprehension section.

3 Although this talk is concerned with increasing reading speed, it is important to be aware that we read at different speeds according to the nature of the text and our purpose in reading. On what occasions, therefore, do we need to read quickly? The ability to read quickly is useful if we wish to read a short passage in a hurry in order to gain an overall impression of it. It is also useful if we want to glance through a text to determine how relevant it is for our purposes or if we want to review a text after first reading it very carefully. The ability to read certain texts quickly is thus especially useful when a student is working largely on his own at, say, sixth form or university level.
Now answer question 3 in the Listening comprehension section.

4 Now let us look at how we read. When we read a printed text, our eyes move across a page in short, jerky movements. We recognise words usually when our

eyes are still – when they fixate. Each time they fixate, we see a word or a group of words. This is known as the recognition span or the visual span. The length of time for which the eyes stop – the duration of the fixation – varies considerably from person to person. It also varies within any one person according to his purpose in reading and his familiarity with the text. Furthermore, it can be affected by such factors as lighting and tiredness.

Now answer question 4 in the Listening comprehension section.

5 Unfortunately, in the past many reading improvement courses have concentrated too much on how our eyes move across the printed page. As a result of this misleading emphasis on the purely visual aspects of reading, numerous exercises have been devised to train the eye to see more words at one fixation. For instance, in some exercises, words are flashed on to a screen for, say, a tenth or a twentieth of a second. Other exercises have required students to fix their eyes on some central point, taking in the words on either side. Such word patterns are often in the shape of rather steep pyramids, constructed so the reader takes in more and more words at each successive fixation. All these exercises are very clever, but it's one thing to improve a person's ability to *see* words and quite another thing to improve his ability to read a text efficiently. Reading requires the ability to understand the relationship between words. Consequently, for these reasons, many experts have now begun to question the usefulness of eye training – especially since any approach which trains a person to read isolated words and phrases would seem unlikely to help him in reading a continuous text.

Now answer question 5 in the Listening comprehension section.

6 What, then, is the best way to improve reading speed when working on one's own? One recommended method is to practise with simple material, stopping at the end of each section or chapter to jot down a few notes. Then reread the appropriate section quickly in order to check your notes. In this way, it may be possible to develop a strategy for dealing with more difficult material. Remember, however, that the chief factors which will contribute to success are a desire to read quickly and the determination to practise reading quickly.

Now answer question 6 in the Listening comprehension section.

C Lecture

Listen carefully to the brief lecture I'm going to give on increasing reading comprehension. Look at the extract when you're asked to do so. Take outline notes of the important points and read carefully through the extract immediately after the lecture.

Increasing reading comprehension

The degree of comprehension and the extent to which you can select information and organise it for your purposes is the most important factor in reading efficiently. We see words with our eyes but we use our brains to select and organise the information conveyed. Words are an integral part of phrases and sentences, depending on – and influencing – the other words in the sentence. Sentences and paragraphs themselves are interrelated. Now a familiarity with the grammatical patterns of the language helps the native speaker to hold words, phrases and sentences in abeyance and to anticipate what will come. The native speaker subconsciously knows when some words and phrases require closer scrutiny than others (and also sentences and paragraphs) and is thus in a position to read quickly.

The ideas expressed in a text are related to one another by various reference and linking devices. Let's take reference devices first. Certain words are used to refer either backwards to words or information given earlier or else forwards to refer to words or information which will follow. The use of pronouns is a good example of reference. If you look at the accompanying extract in your book, Reference 2b, you will see a sentence illustrating this. 'Most students who take detailed notes have little time to reflect on the ideas being communicated. They fail to see the general for a mass of detail.' The pronoun 'They' in the second sentence refers back to 'Most students who take notes'. Incidentally, if you look at 2a, you will see an example of the use of the phrases 'the former' and 'the latter': 'the former' refers back to the students who take no notes and try to listen critically to the lecture, while 'the latter' refers back to the other students who take detailed notes. A reference device may, of course, refer back over several sentences; sometimes it may refer forwards. You will see in the first part of the extract a list of common ways of marking reference – as well as ways of denoting linkage.

Linkage is another important device for showing the relationship between ideas in a text. Words showing linkage, usually referred to as connectives, are important signposts to look for in reading. Look at Extract 1 again: B.1 gives various examples of connectives which denote addition: first within a sentence ('and', 'not only . . . but also', 'as well', and so on) and secondly sentence connectives ('Moreover', 'In addition', 'Furthermore'). The degree of your familiarity with such devices as connectives – as well as reference devices – is an important factor in determining your level of understanding of a written text.

We come now to the question of vocabulary. The number of words you know will affect the ease with which you read. Many students immediately reach out for their dictionaries when they meet a new or an unfamiliar word. Unfortunately, by the time they've found the meaning of the word, they may have forgotten the context in which it appeared. Consequently, they have to go back to the beginning of the sentence – or paragraph – and read it again. Now this practice can be expensive on time, especially when several words have to be looked up. Sometimes, of course, the definition of a word is essential, especially in the physical and social sciences. But on many other occasions the exact definition of a word is relatively unimportant.

When the definition is not so important, a more efficient way of dealing with new vocabulary is to attempt to deduce the meaning of a word from its context. Often there will be at least one clue in the sentence to help you to deduce the meaning of a particular word. Let's take the word 'thade' as an example. Now you don't know what it means because I've just invented it. Listen to this sentence:

    'It's advisable to use thade.'

You still don't know what it means: it could mean 'effort', or indeed, it could even refer to an after-shave lotion. There are simply not enough clues available. Now listen again:

    'It's advisable to use thade in tutorial discussions.'

We still can't deduce its meaning but we can get a little closer. We know it's connected with learning – probably with a technique employed in tutorial discussion. Now listen again:

    'It's advisable to use thade in tutorial discussions. Those students who express radical views strongly and aggressively do not realise that such arguments advanced thadefully receive much more sympathetic attention from their listeners. Indeed, by setting out in apparent agreement and then beginning to

differ a little at first and then more and more, the student is much more
likely to convert his opponents to his way of thinking.'
A dictionary isn't necessary now: 'thade' is the technique of starting off in
agreement with one's opponent and then steadily differing. It is, in fact, used here
to refer to a way of arguing radical views subtly and tactfully. (Don't forget,
however, that 'thade' is a nonsense word: it doesn't really exist.)

A useful way of increasing your vocabulary is to relate one word to another. If
you learn a new word, try to relate it to its appropriate synonyms and antonyms.
Learn words in groups or try at least to associate them with a particular context.
Note the spelling and pronunciation of each new word you meet. Absorb it into
your active vocabulary, using it wherever possible in your discussions and written
work.

Nothing is better than reading practice for improving your vocabulary. Read
and read – provided that you understand what you read. When you find a
particular book very difficult, keep at it and try to apply the methods I've
suggested. Then, for relaxation, put it down and pick up an easier book – perhaps a
simplified reader – and you'll begin to enjoy it.

Unit Five

Lectures

A Listening comprehension

You will hear a short talk on which you will be asked questions. The talk will be divided into sections, after each of which there will be a pause. You will be required to answer one question during each pause. (Turn off your machine while you answer.)

Listening to lectures

1 There are many different types of lectures: at one extreme there are those lectures packed with information while at the other extreme there are those which appear to be pure entertainment. You may expect a lecture to be highly factual and you may be disappointed when this is not so. But the amount of factual information given in a lecture is rarely any indication of the usefulness of that particular lecture. Many university lecturers argue that the chief function of a lecture is to stimulate learning. It should motivate students to think and learn. Indeed, if the purpose of a lecture were simply to convey information, then most textbooks would do this far better.
Now answer question 1 in the Listening comprehension section.

2 Several lecturers digress frequently from the subject of their lecture; a few even give personal reminiscences. You will soon become familiar with the different characteristics of each lecturer and so you will be able to spot such digressions more easily. Familiarity with the subject of the lecture will make it easier to identify salient points. In addition, an awareness of the various devices used to signal information and attitudes will be invaluable in distinguishing the important from the unimportant.
Now answer question 2 in the Listening comprehension section.

3 No matter what the type of lecture and style of delivery, you should attempt to adopt a critical attitude. You should avoid sitting passively or scribbling detailed notes without considering what you're writing. Instead, you should try to think critically and independently.
   Get into the habit of writing down questions to discuss with your colleagues later. Prepare for each lecture by glancing through the notes you took of the previous lecture. If you have the title of the lecture in advance, do some preliminary reading before the lecture. Approach the lecture with as much background knowledge as possible and with a critical attitude.
Now answer question 3 in the Listening comprehension section.

4 It is also vital to carry out any follow-up work that may result from the lecture. Remember to leave a period free as soon as possible afterwards so that you can go through your notes and digest what was said. Then you can make a note of the follow-up reading which you intend to do.

Now answer question 4 in the Listening comprehension section.

5 A small but useful point of detail: if you sit on the back few rows during a lecture you will probably be under a severe handicap unless the acoustics of that particular lecture theatre are exceptional. Why should this apply more to foreign learners than to native speakers? The native speaker is able to make use of fewer clues or signals in order to obtain meaning: so even if he misses certain words, he can still understand the gist of the message. Many foreign learners need every signal possible in order to understand each statement: they must hear every word clearly. And so it's very important to avoid missing any of the cues given and to catch every word spoken. Sitting near the front of the lecture room helps a lot.

Now answer question 5 in the Listening comprehension section.

6 Sometimes you may wonder how much time you ought to spend on lectures, especially as examinations approach. Should you sacrifice a lecture or a seminar in order to do some more reading? A decision of this nature, of course, is highly subjective and impossible to answer in general terms. On certain courses lectures are very important and cover most of the ground for the student. Other lectures may be just as relevant but in a more indirect way, giving the student new ideas and providing necessary motivation. In any case, there is a definite advantage in attending a lecture with the rest of the study group: nothing seems worse than to feel you've missed a lecture which others found important and interesting.

Now answer question 6 in the Listening comprehension section.

Unit Six

Using a dictionary

A Listening comprehension

You'll hear a short talk, on which you'll be asked questions. The talk will be
divided into sections, after each of which there'll be a pause. You'll be required
to answer one question during each pause. (Turn off your machine while you answer.)

What kind of dictionary?

1 A good dictionary is indispensable for all students at all levels. Note the word
'good'. A good English dictionary will tell you precisely and accurately how
words are used. It will *report* usage: it will not prescribe infallible 'rules' about
which words to use and which words not to use. Indeed, there is no institution in
Britain nor in the United States which has the necessary authority to formulate
rules concerning correct and incorrect English. English usage is determined by the
people who use the language – not by any language academy.

Dictionaries, therefore, are based solely on an observation of the standard
language of a community – generally on the language used by educated speakers
and good writers. What are the implications of this? First, as I have said, a
dictionary has no authority to prescribe rules: it simply describes. Secondly, it
will probably not include many of the non-standard elements in the language such
as regional variations. Thirdly, any dictionary will date quickly since the speech
of a community is always changing. Old dictionaries have glaring omissions
and give false information, so make certain that your dictionary is *not* more than
ten or twelve years old.

Now answer question 1 in the Listening comprehension section.

2 Many students use native language-to-English dictionaries: for example, Chinese
to-English, French-to-English, English-to-German, English-to-Arabic, and so on.
Though such dictionaries have a limited use, they do encourage the tendency to
regard each new item in English as having a one-word equivalent in the student's
mother tongue. Take, for example, the word 'simpatico' in Italian: one well-
known Italian–English dictionary gives as English equivalents: 'attractive',
'charming', 'genial', 'nice', 'agreeable', 'congenial'. (È un uomo simpatico = He's
a nice man.) None of these words, however, conveys the exact meaning of the
Italian word. English simply does not possess an equivalent. The converse also
happens. In some languages no equivalent at all exists for certain English words:
take the word 'privacy' for example. The concept of privacy is totally unknown in

Chinese family life: consequently, the nearest equivalent to the English word is
私生活 /siː ʃʌn hwɔ(t)/. But this means 'private life' (as opposed to 'public life')
rather than 'privacy'.

Now answer question 2 in the Listening comprehension section.

3 Several dictionaries have been specially written for foreign learners of English and
are generally simplified. Some – like the *New Method English Dictionary*
(Longman) – are written within a carefully controlled vocabulary. Other
dictionaries give the learner guidance on the context of words. Derivations are
generally excluded from such dictionaries, since they are not of much help to the
foreign learner. Perhaps the most widely known and the most useful dictionary
for the foreign student is the *Advanced Learner's Dictionary* (Oxford University
Press). This dictionary is useful at all stages of learning English. You should,
however, also familiarise yourself with such other well-known dictionaries as the
Shorter Oxford English Dictionary and Webster's *Third New International
Dictionary*. There have also been published fairly recently several subject
dictionaries – the *Penguin Dictionary of Science*, to name but one. You will find
such dictionaries increasingly useful as you begin to specialise in your studies.

Now answer question 3 in the Listening comprehension section.

C Lecture

Listen carefully to the brief lecture I'm going to give on the information contained
in a dictionary. Take outline notes of the important points.

What a dictionary contains

In order to use a dictionary – or any reference book, for that matter – it is first
necessary to understand the alphabetical arrangement of words in English.
Arranging words according to their first letter is fairly straightforward: 'amount',
'bite', 'chance', 'differ' and so on. It's a little more difficult when certain words in a
list begin with the same letter: in such cases, however, the words are arranged
according to their second letters: 'pass', 'personality', 'play', 'post', 'print'. If the
first two letters of a word are the same, the third letter determines the alphabetical
order in which they're placed.

Almost all dictionaries give guide words at the top of each page: these guide
words, often printed in heavy type or large type, can save the reader a great deal of
time in locating a particular word. For example, if you want to find the word
'ingrained', turn over the pages of your dictionary, looking only at the guide words
at the top of each page. If you see 'inflammatory' (I-N-F) on the left-hand side and
'initiate' (I-N-I) on the right-hand side, then you'll know that 'ingrained' (I-N-G)
is given on that particular page.

What information does a dictionary generally contain? First, it gives the spelling
of a word. The English language is notorious for its spelling inconsistencies. A lot
of people – including native speakers of English – attempt to guess the spelling of
words they're not certain about.

Next, a dictionary will give information on syllable division. Separate syllables
are generally indicated by a space between them or by a dash or by a dot. An
awareness of syllable division is useful for writing purposes – that is, for knowing
where to divide a word which occurs at the end of a line and continues on to the
next line. But that's not all. Syllable division, together with stress, is very
important in pronunciation.

Pronunciation is shown either by the use of phonetic symbols or by certain marks called diacritical marks. Although the system employing phonetic symbols is generally the more difficult of the two, it is a more exact guide to pronunciation. In addition, phonetic script is used by a large number of modern dictionaries, while diacritical marks vary from one dictionary to another. The introduction to any dictionary will give a table showing the phonetic symbols or diacritical marks used.

Dictionaries also give information regarding parts of speech. The word 'couple', for example, can be used as a verb or a noun, and so it's marked 'n' and 'v' in most dictionaries. The word spelt P-R-E-S-E-N-T is shown as an adjective (pronounced /'preznt/), a noun (pronounced /'preznt/), and a transitive verb (pronounced /pri'zent/). Also, many dictionaries indicate the principal parts of the verbs listed, especially in the case of irregular verbs, when it's very important for the student to know the past tense and past participle forms. One dictionary for foreign learners, the *Advanced Learner's Dictionary*, shows whether a noun is countable or uncountable. In addition to providing all the information I've indicated, the *Advanced Learner's Dictionary* even indicates the chief patterns of the verbs listed.

It is with the meanings of words that most dictionaries are concerned. When used sensibly, a dictionary will be of enormous assistance in providing the exact meaning of a word for a particular purpose. Many dictionaries give the most common meaning of a word first in any list of meanings: others give the earliest meaning first. It's essential to know your dictionary. Here, for example, are six different meanings listed for the noun 'study' given in the *Advanced Learner's Dictionary*: **1** devotion of time and thought to getting knowledge of, close examination of, a subject, especially from books; **2** something that attracts investigation; **3** *be in a brown study*, musing, unaware of people, happenings, etc near one; **4** room used by somebody (eg in his home) for reading, writing, etc; **5** sketch, etc made for practice or experiment; piece of music played as a technical exercise; **6** (old use) earnest effort.

The particular meaning of a word, then, depends on the context in which it is used.

Finally, a good dictionary will indicate any limitations or special uses of particular words. Certain words listed may be literary or archaic: 'betwixt', for example, is rarely used and the *Advanced Learner's Dictionary* precedes its definition of 'betwixt' with the phrase 'old or literary use'. Other words will be listed as colloquial or slang, and so should be avoided in formal writing.

Before I close, I would like to remind you that in this unit you will see how four dictionaries deal with the same word. When looking up any word in any dictionary, first familiarise yourself with the conventions used and then read carefully the whole of the entry. A dictionary is a most valuable tool in your studies if used carefully and wisely.

Unit Seven

Reading textbooks

A Listening comprehension

You will hear a short talk on which you will be asked questions. The talk will be divided into sections, after each of which there will be a pause. You will be required to answer one question during each pause. (Turn off your machine while you answer.)

Skimming

1 People often skim when they want to look for the gist of a text – that is, its general meaning. However, this is only one reason for skimming – I shall describe others later in this talk. When we use a normal reading approach – whether we read quickly or slowly – we read line by line. But when we skim, we adopt a different approach. Instead of concentrating on each single horizontal line, our eyes are generally aware of a larger area. When we're skimming, our eyes may appear to an onlooker to move vertically down a page or even to hop about in no regular direction. What really happens, however, is that our eyes are regulated by the structure of the text: in other words, they move where the sense dictates. Such movements are also influenced by our purpose in reading and the information we wish to extract from the text.
Now answer question 1 in the Listening comprehension section.

2 We adopt such an approach in skimming because we're primarily interested in speed. We may, for example, want to extract the gist of a particular text in as short a time as possible. This approach will have an effect on the level of our comprehension of the general text. When skimming, we deliberately reconcile ourselves to a lower comprehension level in order to gain something different from the text. We're willing to miss particular details in a text so that we can quickly obtain the information we want. The fact that the time taken to skim a text could well be under half the time taken to read it makes this kind of sacrifice worthwhile for certain purposes.
Now answer question 2 in the Listening comprehension section.

3 When is skimming useful in our studies? We often want to find out what a certain book or article is about and whether it contains anything useful for our purpose. Today it's more important than ever before for the specialist to keep up with the latest developments in his particular field. But, to do this, he has to cope with ever increasing masses of literature – a task which can only be achieved by using the appropriate skimming techniques. Again, in higher education, students are given

long lists of background reading, not all of which will be of equal value. Even the mass of popular literature requires the application of skimming skills. Most of us skim newspapers, magazines, advertisements, and even some kinds of instructions.

Now answer question 3 in the Listening comprehension section.

4 Two particular forms of skimming are scanning and search-reading. We scan when we want to locate *specific* information, usually of a fairly detailed nature. For example, when we want to find out the date of a certain battle in a history textbook, we use the index and then scan the pages referred to until we come across the date we want. Similarly, we scan when we want to find a particular point in a text. The point may take the form of a word, phrase, formula, statement, or series of statements. Scanning is largely a matter of recognition of what we're looking for. Sometimes we may not even follow the order of the text but dart about backwards and forwards within the text. We inspect most of the text very rapidly indeed but occasionally we inspect parts of the text much more closely. Once we've found what we want, we'll probably read the particular statement very carefully to check the information.

Now answer question 4 in the Listening comprehension section.

5 Search-reading (or selective reading) is like scanning in certain ways: we look through a text in order to locate information. This time, however, the process is not quite so simple as the recognition of a word or phrase. We search-read to locate *general* information on a topic rather than to find a particular point. Consequently, we usually (but not always) glance through the text, following the order of the presentation of the information. We inspect the text very rapidly indeed, as in scanning, but alternate such rapid inspection with longer periods of closer inspection of the text. During such periods of close inspection, we'll probably apply ordinary reading techniques.

Now answer question 5 in the Listening comprehension section.

6 Both scanning and search-reading are usually combined with other reading techniques and can be used by fast and slow readers alike. What is important is that readers should be able to vary their speed and approach, and so read more flexibly. The ability to skim, using the techniques mentioned, increases the flexibility of a person's whole approach to reading.

Now answer question 6 in the Listening comprehension section.

Unit Eight

Learning in small groups: Tutorials and seminars

A Listening comprehension

You will hear a short talk, on which you will be asked questions. The talk will be divided into sections, after each of which there will be a pause. You will be required to answer one question during each pause. (Turn off your machine while you answer.)

Improving your speaking ability

1 Although most foreign learners of English at colleges and universities are primarily concerned with improving their ability to read and write English, many also want to speak English more fluently. Unfortunately, however, many students expect to swallow a magic language pill and improve overnight. Progress on a self-study basis may be slow and difficult, but intelligent and systematic practice can lead to an improvement of the oral skills.
   Now answer question 1 in the Listening comprehension section.

2 In addition to practice in speaking, you should try to listen to native speakers of English whenever possible. Films and television programmes are often very useful, but these are not enough by themselves. Active participation on your part is required. Listen closely to tapes and records of English, repeating the sounds whenever possible. Accurate imitation is not as easy as many students think. Listen very closely and practise an exercise several times until you achieve almost perfect pronunciation. Don't listen only once and continue rapidly through the rest of the course or the tape. This is a mistake too many students make. You will get very little benefit if you work quickly and carelessly through oral drills and exercises.
   Now answer question 2 in the Listening comprehension section.

3 Now a word about pronunciation exercises. It's essential that you should be able to hear the correct sounds of English before you try to produce them. For example, if you cannot hear the difference between 'sheep' and 'ship', you'll never be able to distinguish between both sounds in your speech. Therefore, in any pronunciation exercise, first listen carefully and then practise speaking. In this type of exercise, accurate imitation of good models is absolutely essential.
   Now answer question 3 in the Listening comprehension section.

4 When you use words of more than one syllable, you must master the stress pattern of the word. There is no simple rule for knowing which syllable to stress: you must learn the stressing of each word individually. Incorrect stress often makes it harder to understand a word or a sentence than incorrect pronunciation does.

Group stress is very important, too. Again, there are no rules for finding out which syllables to stress in a word group or a sentence. Everything depends on the context – on the meaning intended. For example, in the statement, 'John's WALKing home', the stress on the first syllable of 'walking' denotes that John is not going home by bus or by car. 'John's walking HOME' denotes that he isn't walking to school or to church. Finally, in the statement 'JOHN's walking home', the speaker signifies that it is John – not Robert – who's walking home. Now answer question 4 in the Listening comprehension section.

5 Stress is very closely linked to intonation – the tune of a word group or (if you like) the rise and fall of the voice. You should be familiar with the shapes of the tunes in English, for English intonation will differ from the intonation of your own language. Again, you must listen carefully to samples of English speech. You cannot learn intonation from a book. The shape of a tune depends largely on the attitude you want to express and on the number of important words in the statement. Correct and natural intonation can only be achieved after long practice in speaking and after acquiring a 'feel' for the language.
Now answer question 5 in the Listening comprehension section.

6 So much for the elements of pronunciation. Exercise material and drills are only the beginning. After the initial stages, your ability to talk in English can be developed only by frequent practice in conversation and discussion. You must seize every opportunity to talk – but make sure you've something to say. Emphasis on accuracy of pronunciation and sentence structure should now give way to a desire to *communicate* with success and ease in real-life situations. Indeed, your aim shouldn't be perfection any longer: it's better to make a few mistakes and be understood than to remain silent for fear of making a mistake! Now answer question 6 in the Listening comprehension section.

C Lecture

Listen carefully to the brief lecture I'm going to give on tutorials and seminars. Take outline notes of the important points.

Tutorials and seminars

There is at present some confusion between the terms 'tutorials' and 'seminars'. Many lecturers regard them as interchangeable. Strictly speaking, however, tutorials refer to small groups in which a lecturer or tutor adopts the role of the expert or the authority. Students are generally required to submit assignments for discussion by the tutor and other members of the group. The seminar is also a small group, but it operates at a more advanced level and is generally devoted to a specific aspect of a course, functioning largely on a question-and-answer basis.

A third type of group is the *informal* discussion group, often taking place in the cafeteria or students' common room and arising spontaneously from the student's need to discuss his work. Although discussion in such groups can often degenerate into idle gossip, the potentials of these groups are nevertheless very great. For any such group to operate successfully, the following conditions should be observed. First, at least one member of the group must be reasonably well-informed about the particular topic being discussed. Secondly, the discussion must not be too informal: one student should act as chairman or group leader and make sure that digressions are kept to a minimum. Thirdly, the members of the group must do some reading beforehand.

The tutorial and seminar can be of tremendous benefit to the foreign learner of English once initial shyness and fear have been overcome. On the one hand, however, a student may remain silent because of lack of confidence in handling the language. On the other hand, a student who remains silent throughout a discussion may lack something to say. It's advisable, therefore, that each student prepare as much as possible before the group meets. Indeed, the weaker in English a student is, the more he should prepare the topic for discussion. It's helpful to have something to say, but this is not sufficient. The *desire* to communicate is another factor affecting performance in tutorials. The student should *want* to speak.

It's very important not to worry about losing face and making mistakes in a tutorial. If a student has something useful to say, no one will laugh at him if he makes a mistake of grammar or pronunciation. Most people make such mistakes in their own language without realising it. Far more important than trivial aspects of 'correctness' in tutorials is having something worthwhile to say and the desire to succeed in *communicating* one's ideas. Moreover, each time a student makes a statement that is appropriate for a particular situation, he will be encouraged and gain confidence. Each time he correctly uses a particular word, phrase or sentence structure, it will be reinforced in his mind. *Starting* to speak in a tutorial is generally the hardest task of all. But once accomplished, speaking will become steadily easier.

A strong argument in favour of tutorials and seminars is that they help to develop the oral skills – both in the case of the foreign learner and in the case of the native speaker. Specialists must be trained to present papers and to discuss their work with others. The seminar can be an effective way of developing the language skills required for this type of situation. In addition, by communicating orally, a person is often able to clarify his own thoughts on a particular topic. Finally, oral discussion in small groups provides a good balance to lectures and to reading.

Unit Nine

Writing reports and articles

A Listening comprehension

You will hear a short talk, on which you'll be asked questions. The talk will be divided into sections, after each of which there'll be a pause. You'll be required to answer one or two questions during each pause. (Turn off your machine while you answer.)

Judgement skills in writing

1 Whenever we write anything – a letter, a report, or an article – we generally write with a certain audience in mind. When a topic is set, therefore, the first step is to determine the type of reader for which the material is intended. The scientist who reports an experiment for a fellow scientist will write in an entirely different manner than if he were writing the same report for a layman. When you begin to write a report, be clear about whether you are writing for a colleague, an examiner, a supervisor or a layman. Your audience will influence not only the kind of language used but also the amount of detail you include and the way you develop your argument.

Now answer question 1 in the Listening comprehension section.

2 Faults appearing in many reports relate to style. One particular fault is in the use of conversational forms – particularly in the use of contractions. For example, some students write 'it's' instead of 'it is', 'can't' instead of 'cannot', 'mustn't' instead of 'must not', and so on. Although such contractions may be appropriate in conversation and in informal letter writing, they are out of place in formal report writing. Colloquialisms and slang are also completely out of place in most written English prose: the use of 'kids' for 'children' and 'OK' for 'all right' or 'correct' are just two examples of such usage. Finally, you should avoid using in your written work such clichés as 'To start at the beginning' and 'food for thought' – a fault of many native speakers as well as foreign learners.

Now answer question 2 in the Listening comprehension section.

3 Make sure that every section of your report is relevant. The amount of information you'll gather will generally be far more than the amount you require for your particular purpose. The amount you'll want to reproduce, in fact, will be limited by your title, your purpose in writing, and by the time available. Even important information should be rejected if it's not really relevant.

Now answer questions 3 and 4 in the Listening comprehension section.

4 You will now be concerned with planning and ordering your information. If you can make a rough 'model', it will help you to visualise the various aspects of the subject. Most topics can be divided into sections or parts. Even long reports and theses are best dealt with in this way at first. You must then judge the relative importance of each division and sub-division. Once you've completed your 'model', you'll be ready to start writing out your plan. This will necessitate arranging the items in your 'model' in some kind of sequence – that is, in deciding on the order of presentation. Remember, however, that there are usually several ways of ordering information on a topic, depending on your approach to the subject.

Now answer questions 5 and 6 in the Listening comprehension section.

Unit Ten

Learning and remembering

A Listening comprehension

You will hear a short talk, on which you will be asked questions. The talk will be
divided into sections, after each of which there will be a pause. You will be required
to answer one or two questions during each pause. (Turn off your machine while
you answer.)

Memory

1 'Memory is the thing we forget with.' This schoolboy definition of the term
'memory' is no more absurd than many other existing views of memory. Indeed,
many people still tend to regard memory as something concrete – rather like a leg,
an arm, or the brain. Others view memory as a mental faculty. Certain people are
said to have a good memory; advertisements urge students to take courses to
improve their memory. All such views of memory are quite inaccurate and
misleading.
Now answer question 1 in the Listening comprehension section.

2 The truth is that memory is an *activity*; and, as such, it's virtually inseparable
from the activities of learning and remembering. Professor Ian Hunter, in his
excellent book *Memory** (published by Penguin), refers to three phases of memory.
The initial phase involves an experience or activity – for example, witnessing an
accident, watching a TV programme, attending a lecture. The final phase involves
an experience or an activity that is influenced or made possible by the first phase –
for example, being able to describe the accident in the initial phase or to discuss
the TV programme or the lecture. The intermediate phase involves the retention
of the initial experience or activity until the later phase of remembering. These
three phases are called learning, retaining and remembering.
Now answer questions 2 and 3 in the Listening comprehension section.

3 The learning phase is a complex one, but the more active the learning process, the
more successful the remembering will generally be. The intermediate phase of
memory is in many ways the phase about which the least is known. Since the
effects of the learning are generally neither apparent nor observable during the
retention stage, they can only be inferred from the third phase – from one's
performance in remembering. Remembering, the third phase of memory, involves

*I. Hunter *Memory*. Penguin, 1964.

new experiences and activities resulting from, or influenced by, the initial ones. When we remember particular experiences, there are often gaps in our remembering, differences in the sequencing of the ideas, slight modifications and interpretations. No lecturer ever gives the same lecture twice in exactly the same way each time; even actors reciting parts cannot give two identical performances. Changes occur because remembering is essentially an activity, influenced by a number of complex factors. Many of these factors are determined by previous learning, while others are determined by such factors as present interest, tiredness, nervousness, and so on.

Now answer questions 4 and 5 in the Listening comprehension section.

4 The experiences and activities involved in the process of remembering, therefore, are of necessity different from the initial experiences and activities. This is how a human being differs from a computer. For a start, only a little of the initial experience is remembered. Our purpose and our interests directly influence what we perceive or experience. Consequently, selection is the key factor in these early stages of learning. This is why good notes, based on a critical approach to the material being learnt, are so important as an aid to recall.

Now answer question 6 in the Listening comprehension section.

5 Remembering can take the form of recognition as well as recall. For example, we can recognise a person's face or identify a correct answer. Indeed, one way of seeing if forgetting has really occurred is by means of a recognition test. Even when we think we've forgotten the initial experience, we can often still recognise information based on it. Active recall, however, is generally of far greater value in study than pure recognition or identification. Recall involves reconstructing and reproducing the original material learnt. And so the original is modified not only by our own particular language skills and habits but also by our own experience and way of thinking. Deduction and inference can often help recall. Take, for instance, the case of a person's age. I always forget how old my nephew is, but I remember that I went to live in Hong Kong one year before he was born. The year of my arrival in Hong Kong was 1956, so I can deduce that my nephew was born in 1957. By subtracting 1957 from the present year, I can easily obtain his age.

Now answer question 7 in the Listening comprehension section.

C Lecture

Listen carefully to the brief lecture I'm going to give on methods of improving learning procedures. Take outline notes of the important points.

Methods of improving learning procedures

In spite of the claims of many courses aimed at memory improvement, it's impossible to prescribe any method for improving memory in general. Long periods of practice in memorising don't improve learning. Instead of asking how memory can be improved we should seek to improve learning procedures.

The first step in any procedure should be to survey the material for learning. The organisation of the learning task itself will depend on certain factors. What's the nature of the material to be learnt? What's to be remembered? And what is to be ignored? What's the purpose of remembering? How much has the initial material been understood? All these factors will determine the way in which the material is organised for learning. The next step in the procedure is the selection of the relevant from the less relevant and the structuring of the material to be learnt. The more clearly arranged the material is, the better it's learnt. Having carefully considered the purpose for which our notes are to be used, for example, we should then select and arrange the notes systematically. Each note in a set of outline notes will trigger off other ideas, related to, and interdependent on, one another.

An important aspect in organising learning is the attempt to learn by wholes. This will necessitate working from a general plan of the material and may even require some rearrangement of the material. Certainly, the whole is generally more meaningful than the individual parts, some of which will be irrelevant or will produce a chain of irrelevant associations. Emphasis on the whole rather than on the separate parts guards against a lack of perspective and prevents too much attention being paid to any one particular aspect. Some psychologists – Mace included – suggest that the natural order of learning is from the general to the particular, advocating learning by the 'whole' method rather than dividing the material into sections. Clearly, certain sections or aspects of a topic will require more attention than others: however, allowing for such modifications, learning by wholes is considered by many to be the most efficient way of learning. Thus, for example, the learning of individual signs in note-taking is much better accomplished when considered in the context of the perception of relationships and the total note-taking skills. By working from the whole, it's possible to see how one point is dependent on another, taking on additional meaning in relation to that point.

This raises the whole question of the use of associations in learning. Before dealing with highly meaningful associations, I want to say a few words about mnemonic and other artificial systems of memorising. Alexander Laing in his book *The Art of Study** quotes a good example of a mnemonic which has often been given to medical students to help them to remember the cranial nerves:

'Oh! Oh, Mama! Papa Took A Fork And Gave Pony Some Hay.'
Because this sentence is so ridiculous, it's not difficult to remember it as a mnemonic for: Olfactory, Optic, Motor oculi, Pathetic, Trifacial, Abducent, Facial, Auditory, Glosso-pharyngeal, Pneumogastric, Spinal accessory, and Hypoglossal.

Mnemonics and such devices may be of some use when more meaningful associations don't exist. However, material is generally much more successfully retained if meaningful and logical associations can be made. Often one idea is linked to another idea. Once the material to be learnt has been systematised or structured, the whole range of interrelationships and associations will become apparent. Moreover, ways of relating material usually rely on the most significant or important characteristics of that material.

Material that has to be learnt by heart should be very carefully selected and limited as much as possible. Learning by heart is best if confined to very short periods of study and if combined with other more meaningful and interesting aspects of study. Clearly, it's necessary to learn facts in every subject: principles and formulae in science, dates in history, items of vocabulary in language, verse in literature, quotations, and so on. Constant attempts to recall the particular facts being learnt are far more useful than simple repetition. In this sense, over-learning is desirable. Over-learning refers to being able to recall material correctly and then practising recalling it still more times. We over-learn the alphabet and

*A Laing *The Art of Study*. University of Leeds, 1974.

multiplication tables. Material that has been over-learnt is retained and recalled much more easily than material that has just been sufficiently learnt.

One final point: we can remember anything better if we're interested in it and learn it with the intention of remembering it. It was Sigmund Freud who suggested that we forget because we want to. The corollary is also true: we remember because we want to and because we intend to.

Unit Eleven

Examinations

A Listening comprehension

You'll hear a short talk on which you'll be asked questions. The talk will be divided into sections, after each of which there'll be a pause. You'll be required to answer one or two questions during each pause. (Turn off your machine while you answer.)

Preparing for the examination

1 Preparation for an examination should be started at the outset of the course. The syllabus and book lists, together with past examination papers, help to show the ground covered in a course. Past examination papers also often have the advantage of clearly indicating the type of examination which will be set. You should take a careful note of the number of papers to be taken, the different areas covered by each paper, and the number of questions on each paper. Find out the degree of choice available to candidates; group together all the questions relating to the same topic and draw up a list of the *topics* covered. Finally, check the present syllabus with both the previous syllabus and the previous examination, noting very carefully any changes in the course.
Now answer question 1 in the Listening comprehension section.

2 When the examination eventually approaches, look at the past examination papers again – but this time in far greater detail. It's no longer enough to survey the past examination paper superficially. Most students only glance at past papers, telling themselves that they can answer (say) questions 3 and 4 very well, and 5, 7, 9 and 10 reasonably well, 12 with some difficulty but not 1, 2, 6, 8 and 11. Such a superficial approach gives no true indication at all of what you can do. Instead, look carefully at each question and write outline notes and plans: in this way, you'll soon be able to detect possible weak areas in your knowledge. Occasionally, you should try writing out an answer in full: this is useful practice.
Now answer question 2 in the Listening comprehension section.

3 Frequent and regular periods devoted to revision are far more useful than last-minute attempts to revise. Regular tests and assignments can be of great help because they necessitate a systematic approach to study, distributing the revision work evenly throughout the course. If regular tests and assignments are not a feature of your particular course, try to set aside some time each week for revision – preferably within a few days of the original learning. The revision, however,

should not be limited to repetition or rereading. Active revision, involving recall, frequently necessitates a reorganisation of the initial material and so demands a thorough understanding of everything that has been learned. Indeed, few examination questions will require you to reproduce information in exactly the same way in which it was learned. So, in your revision rethink the material learned, ask questions and reorganise it. Be prepared to write out revised versions of your notes, bringing the original ones up to date and modifying them in the light of your later learning.

Now answer questions 3 and 4 in the Listening comprehension section.

4 Frequent discussions with other students can be of great benefit when revising, especially when taking place in small groups. The different interests of the participants in each group, as well as their different strengths and weaknesses, will add to the learning and provide some kind of balance. It's possible for such a group to prepare a 'mock' examination paper as a trial. Students are thus given the chance of answering questions which are completely new to them and later of discussing them.

Now answer question 5 in the Listening comprehension section.

Unit Twelve

Reference and research techniques

A Listening comprehension

You will hear a short talk on which you will be asked questions. The talk will be divided into sections, after each of which there will be a pause. You'll be required to answer 1 or 2 questions during each pause. (Turn off your machine while you answer.)

Reference techniques: Using a library

1 Although most students are familiar with school and college libraries, few are aware of the many facilities available. The organisation of most libraries, big or small, however, is basically the same. In addition to the newspapers and journals which many stock, all the books in a library are classified in two ways. There are those books which can be borrowed by an authorised user of the library and those which are reference works and cannot be taken out of the library. Reference books – generally encyclopaedias, yearbooks, handbooks, dictionaries, atlases, bibliographies – are considered too widely used to be permitted to leave most libraries. Now answer question 1 in the Listening comprehension section.

2 The first feature of any library with which the student must become completely familiar is the classification system used. The two most common systems in general use are the Dewey decimal system and the Library of Congress system. The Dewey system of classification divides the various fields of knowledge into ten main classes, each denoted by a number: 000–099, General Works; 100–199, Philosophy; 200–299, Religion; 300–399, Social Sciences; 400–499, Language; 500–599, Pure Science; and so on. Take 300 Social Science, for example; 310 denotes books on Statistics, 320 Politics, 330 Economics, 340 Law, 350 Administration, 360 Associations and Institutions, 370 Education, 380 Commerce and Communications, 390 Customs, Costume and Folklore. Further sub-divisions are then made: for example, 370 Education (General), 371 Teachers and Teaching, 372 The Child and School (Primary Education, etc), 373 Secondary Education, 374 General Studies in Adult Education, 375 Curriculum (General), and so on. However, this system is not without obvious weaknesses because certain sections take little account of geographical and cultural factors. Many colleges and universities overseas modify the system slightly in order to meet their own special requirements.
Now answer questions 2 and 3 in the Listening comprehension section.

3 The Library of Congress Classification system, based not on numbers but on

letters of the alphabet, divides the fields of knowledge into twenty broad
categories: A General Works – Polygraphy, B Philosophy – Religion, C History –
Auxiliary Sciences, D History and Topography (excluding America) and so on.
Arabic numerals are then used for further divisions and sub-divisions – rather
like the Dewey system.
Now answer question 4 in the Listening comprehension section.

4 Whatever system of classification is used, it's necessary to rely on the library
catalogue for much of our preliminary information. There are four types of
catalogues in many libraries: the first catalogue to approach is generally the
Index of Subject Headings: this is arranged according to the titles of subjects and
is in alphabetical order: Education is under E, Language is under L, and so on.
Having obtained the numbers of the category into which our subject falls, we
must now look at the Classified Catalogue to find the actual titles of books listed.
Again, the cards are arranged in order for each sub-section, this time according
to the classification numbers. Within each sub-section cards are arranged
alphabetically by the author's name. Detailed information about each book
is generally given here: the publisher, the date of publication, the price, the
number of pages, and so on. Next the Author Catalogue lists each book under the
name of its author. The same detailed information as that found in the Classified
Catalogue is given here. The Title Catalogue in a library is usually incorporated in
the Author Catalogue. The arrangement here is by the first word (or occasionally
the key word) in the title, and the information given is generally the same as that
given on the equivalent card in the Author Catalogue.
Now answer questions 5 and 6 in the Listening comprehension section.

C Lecture

Listen carefully to the brief lecture I'm going to give on research techniques. Take
outline notes of the important points.

Research techniques: Planning and conducting research

The activity of research can be engaged in at any level from the primary school
upwards. A person who is deeply interested in a particular subject or a hobby will
often try to extend his knowledge beyond the bounds of books and established
knowledge. Research is, perhaps, best defined as being a systematic and thorough
enquiry into questions which have a certain significance and importance for the
person involved in a particular field. The results of this enquiry will contribute to
the enlargement of knowledge on the one hand and to a better appreciation of the
issues involved on the other hand.

Research work of any kind comprises two main divisions: the first division con-
cerns the acquisition of knowledge while the second involves progressing beyond
books and establishing new ideas. Now let's examine the actual stages of a research
project – assuming that the necessary specialist knowledge has been acquired.

The first stage in undertaking research of any kind is to select a suitable area for
study. Several topics will probably seem to be available to the student who has
read fairly extensively and who has thought deeply about the subject. If this is the
case, it's advisable to write down a list of all the suitable topics which spring to
mind. Each topic should then be examined carefully. If possible, wait a few weeks
before compiling a short list of topics. Next, consult your tutor or a colleague and
discuss each of the topics short-listed. Your tutor will probably be in a position to

ask the right kind of questions – even though he himself may have little idea of the answers. A good library is generally essential for this stage since a thorough survey of the material available will prevent you from imagining that there are gaps in existing knowledge where, in fact, none really exist.

Next, define the problem as clearly and as concisely as possible. You may wish to change or modify the actual statement of the problem later, but it's essential at this stage to formulate the problem in just the right way, as the whole success of your research will depend on your definition of the problem. The problem should be defined in such a way that a conclusion can be reached and the research accomplished. Too many incomplete research projects lie on shelves because the initial problem was not sufficiently clearly defined.

The third stage is concerned with making observations and collecting data. It's helpful to read research papers concerning related areas of study since, in addition to obtaining peripheral information of use, you will form a good idea of the different methods of setting up various research projects and of treating the results. A card-index system or a loose-leaf notebook is a useful means of recording the information obtained from all your reading.

The data collected should now be examined and analysed. You will then be in a position to formulate tentative hypotheses. Your hypotheses, in turn, will largely determine the method, size and nature of your sampling. Many research workers start out by deliberately avoiding making any predictions. The reason for adopting such an attitude is that the results of the experiment or investigation are then less likely to be influenced by the research worker's existing views or bias.

I mentioned sampling a moment ago. Sampling, whether for a pilot project or for your investigation proper, is essential in many fields of research, since it's clearly impossible to test out a hypothesis on all the people concerned – that is, on the total population. Your sample, therefore, must be accurate and must truly represent the total population with which the research is concerned. Unless random sampling methods are used, great care must be taken to ensure that the sample really *is* representative and that all external factors are excluded.

The investigation is then conducted or the experiment mounted, all relevant data being collected and examined carefully. Many research projects put great emphasis on the statistical analysis of the data. Since it's imperative that the research be conducted objectively, it's only to be expected that most hypotheses rely on statistical evidence for their confirmation or rejection. Statistics, however, are open to abuse and don't always measure the facts under examination. Often they're distorted through chance and other external factors. At other times, they're influenced by prejudice and bias. So, while not actually containing inaccurate information, they may nevertheless convey a misleading picture of the situation through faults of omission and undue emphasis.

To return to the collection and analysis of the data gathered: once this stage has been completed, the results must be interpreted. It's to be hoped that the results will not only bear out the original hypothesis but will also contribute much more to it and involve certain modifications and additions.

The final stage is the writing of the report or thesis. The report should first be written in draft form, for there will be many more modifications than originally foreseen. During the long and difficult period of writing the thesis, you should always keep your audience and purpose firmly in mind. The ability to communicate your findings is just as important as any of the other stages in your research work.